CW00640952

...ed
...ds,
...el.

...ur
...ts
...d,
...of
...experience and a passion for travel.

**Rely on Thomas Cook as your
travelling companion on your next trip
and benefit from our unique heritage.**

Thomas Cook **pocket** guides

GUERNSEY

Written by Lindsay Hunt, updated by Anwer Bati

Published by Thomas Cook Publishing
A division of Thomas Cook Tour Operations Limited
Company registration no. 3772199 England
The Thomas Cook Business Park, Unit 9, Coningsby Road,
Peterborough PE3 8SB, United Kingdom
Email: books@thomascook.com, Tel: +44 (0) 1733 416477
www.thomascookpublishing.com

Produced by Cambridge Publishing Management Limited
Burr Elm Court, Main Street, Caldecote CB23 7NU
www.cambridgepm.co.uk

ISBN: 978-1-84848-400-9

© 2006, 2008 Thomas Cook Publishing
This third edition © 2011
Text © Thomas Cook Publishing,
Maps © Thomas Cook Publishing/PCGraphics (UK) Limited
Based on data © Coast Media Limited

Series Editor: Karen Beaulah
Production/DTP: Steven Collins

Printed and bound in Spain by GraphyCems

Cover photography © Eye Ubiquitous/Alamy

CONTENTS

WHAT'S IN YOUR GUIDEBOOK?

Independent authors Impartial, up-to-date information from our travel experts who meticulously source local knowledge.

Experience Thomas Cook's 165 years in the travel industry and guidebook publishing enriches every word with expertise you can trust.

Travel know-how Thomas Cook has thousands of staff working around the globe, all living and breathing travel.

Editors Travel-publishing professionals, pulling everything together to craft a perfect blend of words, pictures, maps and design.

You, the traveller We deliver a practical, no-nonsense approach to information, geared to how you really use it.

● *Boats at rest in St Peter Port*

INTRODUCTION
Getting to know Guernsey

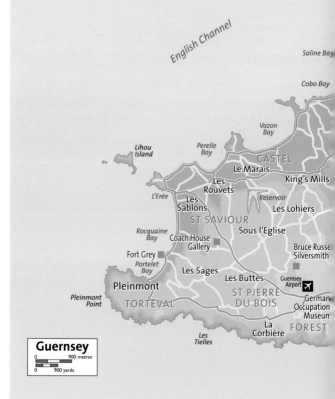

........POI
——— .....Main Road
....Minor Road
✈ ....Airport

English Channel

Saline Bay

Cobo Bay

Vazon Bay

Lihou Island

Perelle Bay

CASTEL

Le Marais

King's Mills

Les Rouvets

L'Erée

Les Sablons

Reservoir

Les Lohiers

ST SAVIOUR

Sous l'Eglise

Rocquaine Bay

Coach House Gallery

Bruce Russel Silversmith

Fort Grey

Portelet Bay

Les Sages

Les Buttes

Guernsey Airport ✈

Pleinmont

ST PIERRE DU BOIS

Pleinmont Point

TORTEVAL

German Occupation Museum

La Corbière

FOREST

Les Tielles

Guernsey

0   900 metres
0   900 yards

N

L'Ancresse Bay

Mont Cuet

Pembroke Bay

Beaucette Marina

Ladies Bay

La Moye

Les Closios

Le Grand Havre

VALE

Les Vardes

Portinfer

rt Soif

L'Islet

Guernsey Freesia Centre

Bordeaux

Bordeaux Harbour

Dehus

Grandes Rocques

Oatlands Village

Saltpans

St Sampson Harbour

Vingtaine de l'Epine

VALE

Capelles

ST SAMPSON

New Marina

Cobo

Saumarez Park & Folk Museum

Telephone Museum

Belle Greve Bay

Le Villocq

ST PETER PORT

St Peter Port

St Peter Port Harbour

Havelet Bay

ST ANDREW

Guernsey Clockmakers

Catherine Best Studio

Fort George

Guernsey Aquarium

Little Chapel

Les Hubits

Soldier's Bay

German Underground Hospital

Sausmarez Manor

Fermain Point

Fermain Bay

La Gran'mère du Chimquière

Calais

Le Bourg

La Villette

ST MARTIN

La Fosse

Petit Port

Moulin Huet Pottery

Jerbourg Point

Petit Bot

Icart

Saints Bay

St Martin's Point

UK

Guernsey

France

Getting to know Guernsey

Guernsey island, along with Herm, Sark and Alderney, which together form the Bailiwick of Guernsey, attract thousands of visitors every year, and it's easy to see why. All the islands have an extraordinarily leisurely way of life, beautiful countryside and waterfront buildings, and dramatic coastlines and bays. They also share a colourful heritage – dating from Neolithic times and including buildings and artefacts from the Norman and Napoleonic eras, and World War II – fabulous seafood and some of the friendliest people you will ever meet.

Finding Guernsey isn't easy on most maps. In the Bay of St Malo, 48 km (30 miles) from the coast of Normandy, it is much closer to France than to the UK, and a good bit warmer and sunnier. On a European scale, Guernsey, and even more so Herm, Sark and Alderney, look minute, but size isn't everything. In fact, the small scale of this seductive archipelago is all part of their appeal.

The islands, along with their close Channel Island neighbour, Jersey, are all subtly different destinations, which serve up a tantalising variety of flavours.

GUERNSEY

Guernsey is the second largest of the Channel Islands, after Jersey. Although densely populated, it feels quiet and intimate. It has stacks of charm, especially along its pretty, cliff-fringed southern coastline and in its delightful capital, St Peter Port. Excellent historic sights, shops and craft centres throughout the island add to its attractions. It even has its own little island, Lihou, which is an absolute haven of peace and an important conservation area. The island was purchased by the States of Guernsey in January 1995. Visitors to Guernsey can cross a causeway from the L'Erée headland at low water to reach Lihou – but always check the tide tables before doing so, because at this point, the tide comes in at an alarming rate.

Guernsey's coastline is rugged and beautiful

GUERNSEY TOWNS

St Peter Port is the hub of life on Guernsey island. A cosmopolitan harbour town typified by its historic buildings, cobbled streets and a marina with yachts gently rocking in the swell, it offers a sophisticated atmosphere, several enticing events (particularly nautical ones), excellent shopping and fine dining.

Guernsey itself has a number of parishes, each with their own character. St Sampson is the industrial heart of the island, while Vale, Castel and St Saviour have some of the finest beaches and headlands. St Pierre du Bois (St Peter in the Wood) and Torteval revel in dramatic coastlines, but the parishes of Forest and St Martin tend to have more sheltered bays and beaches, making them ideal for novice swimmers. Inland, St Andrew has outstanding countryside.

The islands of Herm, Sark and Alderney each offer a different look on life, and can be reached by ferry, or for Alderney, by light aircraft.

1066 AND ALL THAT. . .

The French call the Channel Islands 'Les Îles Anglo-Normandes'. They once formed part of the Duchy of Normandy, and passed into English hands with William the Conqueror. When King John lost control of his Norman possessions in 1204, the Channel Islands were given the choice of reverting to France or remaining English. Shrewdly, they opted for the English side, on condition that they retained their own government and their ancient feudal privileges, relics of which they still hold today. But even now, some islanders still speak the local patois, a form of French intelligible only to their neighbours in Normandy.

Thus the Channel Islands are British Isles, but they are not part of the United Kingdom. They have their own government and culture, their own laws and customs – even their own currency, postal services and tax systems. They bear allegiance to the Crown, but not to Westminster, nor to Brussels – the Channel Islands are not full members of the EU. For the Channel Islanders, the British monarch is still the Duke of Normandy, and when they drink a loyal toast, they raise their glasses to 'The Queen, Our Duke'. But age-old rivalries still exist between the islands, especially between Jersey and Guernsey – each took separate sides in the English Civil War (1642). For over a thousand years the Channel Islands have been subjected to invasion, or threats of invasion. All around the coastline, the islanders have tried to ward off the danger by building fortresses and watchtowers, particularly during the Napoleonic Wars.

SEIGNEURS AND DAMES

The Norman feudal system, in which parcels of land were granted by the king in exchange for military service, has long since lapsed on the larger islands. But some of the ancient manor houses remain, and a few are still inhabited by descendants of the original seigneurial families, such as Sausmarez Manor on Guernsey, or St Ouen's Manor on neighbouring Jersey. You can visit both of these, and find out more. Sark tantalises political historians as – until 2007 – the last remaining feudal society in Europe, still with its Seigneur or Dame as ruler, in name if no longer in practice. By one of those odd paradoxes so typical of the Channel Islands, however, it was never actually feudal in feudal times. Its seigneurial system started only in 1565 but, as the first democratic elections took place in 2008, it can now claim to be the newest democracy in Europe.

WORLD WAR II

World War II is an unforgettable period in Guernsey's history, as it, along with its neighbouring islands, was the only part of the British Isles to be invaded by the Germans. The Occupation story is told in two museums on the island, and visitors often find them fascinating. Don't forget to look at the liberation monuments as well. You'll find Guernsey has an imaginative and very moving monument in St Peter Port (near the Clock Tower by the harbour), where the first German bombs fell in 1940. There are German fortifications around the coasts of the islands.

BEATING THE TAXMAN

Low taxation makes Guernsey, Alderney, Sark and Herm, plus their neighbouring island of Jersey, extremely attractive for wealthy settlers; millionaires queue to live there. If you win the lottery next week and

⬤ *Herm is proud of its Shell Beach*

decide to become a tax exile, you may find resident status is an elusive and protracted goal. For holiday visitors, though, the lower costs of some items, especially jewellery, electrical goods, alcohol, car hire and petrol, give the islands that extra sparkle.

THE OTHER CHANNEL ISLANDS

Jersey is the big one, 14 km (9 miles) across at its widest, basking in southerly sunshine like a glamorous bathing belle. It's a wealthy place, and its residents enjoy the good life in smart restaurants and yacht marinas. Well endowed with superb beaches and high-profile tourist attractions, it has a surprising amount of unspoilt rural scenery too, criss-crossed by a web of tiny lanes. Jersey has more organised entertainment and nightlife than the other islands.

Alderney is the third largest of the Channel Islands and is a self-governing, democratic territory. It is less populous than Guernsey and lies around 37 km (23 miles) northeast of the island. Its geography keeps it free of mass tourism so it has a special appeal for lovers of peace and quiet, birdwatching and open spaces.

Herm is tiny, measuring just 2.5 km (1½ miles) long and 1 km (½ mile) wide, with gorgeous beaches and a charmingly rural interior. Its appeal far outweighs its diminutive size and many devotees find the absence of contrived amusements a distinct advantage. Under the careful supervision of its tenant managers, it promises a tranquil, civilised retreat for a day trip – or longer.

Sark, similarly, has glorious scenery and its winsome feudal customs make it an instant hit with visitors. You can easily see it on a day trip, as thousands do, but it is even better if you stay at one of its excellent hotel-restaurants. There are two privately owned islands in these waters too. Jethou is off the coast of Herm and Brecqhou is at Sark, although these can't be visited – unless you're invited.

THE BEST OF GUERNSEY

TOP 10 ATTRACTIONS

- **The coastline** Walking, driving or cycling around the coast, and discovering some of Guernsey and its neighbouring islands' many beautiful and unspoilt beaches and bays is a must.

- **St Peter Port** Even if you don't visit any of the formal sights, take a stroll around the picturesque streets, perhaps pausing for a spot of shopping or a seafood lunch in one of the many attractive seafront restaurants (see pages 18–23).

- **Hauteville House** People come from around the world, particularly France, to visit the fine house in which Victor Hugo wrote his famous work, *Les Misérables* (see page 20).

- **Castle Cornet** This 13th-century waterfront fortress, with historical, maritime and military museums, is a landmark on Guernsey (see pages 18 and 20).

- **Fort Grey** This Martello tower at Rocquaine Bay contains the fascinating Shipwreck Museum, showing the perils of Guernsey's reef-strewn west coast (see page 32).

- **Sausmarez Manor** is a fine mansion with beautiful gardens that will appeal to all ages (see page 38).

- **German Occupation Museum** Situated close to Le Bourg, in the south, the museum recounts Guernsey's period of Occupation with authentic displays of World War II memorabilia (see page 31)

- **La Valette Underground Military Museum** Housed in a series of German wartime tunnels, this award-winning display of Occupation memorabilia is particularly atmospheric (see page 20).

- **La Coupée** A breathtaking neck of rock links Little Sark to the main island of Sark and is just wide enough for a tractor or horse and cart. It has dizzying drops, and stunning views, to either side (see page 90).

- **Herm** Just a 20-minute ferry ride from St Peter Port, Herm makes the perfect day (or half-day) trip if you want peace, quiet and beautiful surroundings (see page 82).

St Martin's Church

SYMBOLS KEY

The following symbols are used throughout this book:

ⓐ address ❶ telephone ⓦ website address ⓔ email

❹ opening times ❶ important

The following symbols are used on the maps:

𝒊	information office	⭕	city
✉	post office	⭕	large town
🛍	shopping	○	small town
✈	airport	■	point of interest
✚	hospital	—	main road
🛡	police station	—	minor road
🚍	bus station	—	railway
✝	church		
❶	numbers denote featured cafés, restaurants & evening venues		

RESTAURANT CATEGORIES

The symbol after the name of each restaurant listed in this guide
indicates the price of a typical three-course meal without drinks
for one person:

£ under £25   ££ £25–45   £££ over £45

▶ *The western coast of Guernsey can be magical at sunset*

RESORTS
Places under the sun

St Peter Port

In any Channel Island town beauty contest, Guernsey's St Peter Port wins hands down. The whole place focuses on the reclaimed waterfront. Ferries and fishing boats chug purposefully between the bristling jetties, while the halyards of the leisure boats clank in the breeze.

From the sea, St Peter Port's townscape of tall granite houses rising against wooded hillsides seems enmeshed in a cat's cradle of masts and maritime rigging. Exploring the picturesque old town takes you through steep cobbled streets linked by flights of steps, with plenty of good shops en route, as well as the fascinating Town Church. Just by the main harbour car park is Guernsey's Memorial Mast – a tall, white mast celebrating the island's nautical heritage, and near it is the Liberation Monument.

There's a lively cultural feel to St Peter Port, too, with theatre and music venues as well as local craft centres and art galleries to visit. Don't forget to seek out Victor Hugo's home, the fascinating Hauteville House. St Peter Port is the hub of life on Guernsey, so it's fitting that one of the island's largest community projects of recent years is on view here. The Guernsey Tapestry is housed in a purpose-built gallery in the Dorey Centre, next to the 19th-century church of St James the Less. Made by residents of Guernsey as a Millennium project, the tapestry comprises panels covering a century each, which collectively tell of 1,000 years of local history. It is well worth seeing if you visit St Peter Port.

THINGS TO SEE & DO

Castle Cornet

A major land- and seamark, the 13th-century waterfront fortress contains historical, maritime and military museums. Constructed in King John's reign, it was last used for defensive purposes by the Germans in World War II. At midday, red-coated retainers fire an artillery salute from the Royal Battery. The castle also has four gardens based on styles ranging from the 16th to the 19th century, and hosts several events and performances throughout the year.

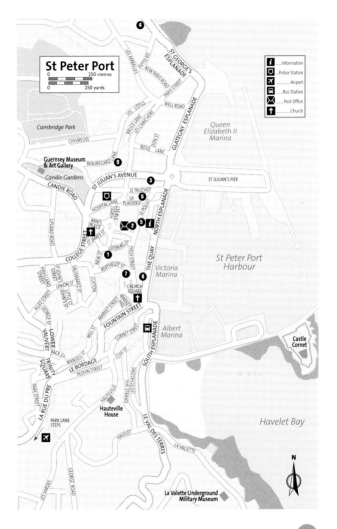

ⓐ Castle Emplacement ⓣ 01481 721657 ⓦ www.museums.gov.gg
ⓛ 10.00–17.00 daily (Apr–Oct) ❶ Admission charge

Guernsey Museum & Art Gallery

An excellent introduction to the history of the island from Neolithic times, including an audiovisual show. Notice the pretty Victorian bandstand incorporated into the museum, and Victor Hugo's statue in the surrounding park. The Rona Cole gallery is the venue for special exhibitions. The shop, café and gardens are free to enter.

ⓐ Candie Gardens ⓣ 01481 726518 ⓦ www.museums.gov.gg
ⓛ 10.00–17.00 daily (summer); 10.00–16.00 daily (winter)
❶ Admission charge

Hauteville House (Victor Hugo's home)

The French writer lived as a political refugee in St Peter Port during 1855–70, when he wrote his epic novel, *Les Misérables*. Guided tours only for the house, which is actually owned by the city of Paris. You can enjoy the garden without charge.

ⓐ Hauteville ⓣ 01481 721911 ⓛ 12.00–16.00 Mon–Sat, closed Sun (Apr); 10.00–16.00 Mon–Sat, closed Sun (May–Sept); tours (45 mins)
❶ Admission charge

La Valette Underground Military Museum

Housed in a series of German wartime tunnels, this award-winning display of Occupation memorabilia is particularly atmospheric and worth a visit.

ⓐ La Valette ⓣ 01481 722300 ⓛ 10.00–17.00 daily (summer)
❶ Admission charge

❶ An excellent-value combined ticket is available for four of Guernsey's most interesting historic sights: Castle Cornet, Guernsey Museum, the Telephone Museum (see page 29) and Fort Grey (see page 32).

TAKING A BREAK

Duke of Normandie £ ❶ Attractively renovated 18th-century hotel-pub
with a good range of wines and bar lunches in a nostalgic maritime
setting, with oak beams, open fire and courtyard barbecue. ❸ Lefebvre
Street ❸ 01481 721431 Ⓦ www.dukeofnormandie.com ⓐ 12.00–14.00,
18.00–21.00 daily

Pelican's Café £ ❷ Modern décor and friendly service in this
smart coffee shop that serves unpretentious fare with a touch of
sophistication. ❸ 24 Le Pollet ❸ 01481 713636 ⓐ 08.00–17.00 Mon–Sat,
closed Sun ❶ No credit cards

The Swan £–££ ❸ This old pub serves hearty helpings of good-value
traditional and more modern dishes, both downstairs and in the stylish
upstairs dining room. The bar menu is available upstairs, as well as

⬥ *St Peter Port's waterfront*

downstairs at lunch, but there is a more sophisticated menu upstairs in the evening. ⓐ St Julian's Avenue ❶ 01481 728969 🕐 12.00–14.00, 18.00–22.00 daily

Absolute End ££ ❹ Award-winning seafood cooking on the seafront, just north of St Peter Port. Good-value set lunches. Attentive, polished service. ⓐ Longstore ❶ 01481 723822 🕐 Lunch and dinner daily, times vary in winter

Christie's ££ ❺ Stylish brasserie in the old town, overlooking the waterfront. Ideal for coffee and cakes, an early-evening drink or a full meal. Specials with oriental and Mediterranean flavours. Live jazz most evenings. ⓐ Le Pollet ❶ 01481 726624 🕐 08.00–22.00 daily

Da Nello ££ ❻ Intimate candlelit dining room offering classic Italian cooking and lots of seafood. Charcoal grills and pastas. Courteous, practised service. ⓐ 46 Le Pollet ❶ 01481 721552 🕐 12.00–14.00, 18.30–22.00 daily

Dix-Neuf Brasserie ££ ❼ Urbane bar-cum-brasserie in a modern setting. Young, friendly staff and lively music. Everything from chic Mediterranean specials to English breakfasts or sticky toffee pudding, but pleasant just for a drink, too. ⓐ 19 Commercial Arcade ❶ 01481 723455 🕐 08.30–24.00 daily (winter times vary)

Mora ££ ❽ Whether you eat a light lunch downstairs, or a fuller meal (lunch and dinner) upstairs, you will be impressed by the quality of cooking and service in this smart restaurant, which draws its inspiration from the produce and dishes of the southwest coast of Britain, the Channel Islands themselves, Normandy and Brittany. ⓐ The Quay ❶ 01481 715053 🕐 12.00–14.15, 18.30–22.00 daily

La Frégate £££ ❾ For a treat, book a table in this elegant hotel-restaurant at the top of St Peter Port. Panoramic views of the town and

SHOPPING

Shopping in St Peter Port is a delight. Waterfront stores cater for visiting yachtsmen, while shops in the steep cobbled streets behind display a mouthwatering VAT-free range of classy clothes, jewellery, cameras, electrical goods, perfumes and shoes.

If you have children to amuse, be sure to visit the National Trust's quaint Victorian shop and parlour (🅰 26 Cornet Street) where costumed ladies sell sweets in jars, or **Guernsey Toys** (🅰 Victoria Road) for a genuine Guernsey teddy.

If antiques interest you, stroll up **Mill Street** and **Mansell Street**, lined with bygones and bric-a-brac, and tempting collectibles. And be sure to have a look at the completely renovated old market behind the parish church, which is now more of a shopping mall, but you can still find flowers, seafood, local meat, fruit and veg, and other produce on sale.

harbour, and memorable French cuisine. 🅰 Les Cotils 🕓 01481 724624 🕒 12.00–14.00, 19.00–21.30 daily ❗ Smart dress required

AFTER DARK

Nightlife on Guernsey is relatively quiet. Local licensing laws permit pubs to open 10.00–00.45 Monday–Saturday, 12.00–00.45 Sundays. There are two cinemas, one in St Peter Port's **Beau Séjour Leisure Centre** (🕓 01481 747210) and a multi-screen complex at **La Mallard**, a former hotel near the airport (🕓 01481 266366). Beau Séjour also stages drama productions in summer. The **St James Concert Hall,** a converted church in St Peter Port (🕓 01481 711360) hosts a range of concerts and other cultural events – details are available from the tourist office or at your hotel. Castle Cornet also has an outdoor theatre, and hosts several musical and other events in season. For later and racier nightlife, try the nightclubs located on **Le Pollet** in the centre of town.

St Sampson & Vale

The northern tip of Guernsey is low-lying and peaceful, despite being quite densely populated (in parts at least). Much land lies under greenhouse glass, or water catchment systems. Here, too, is Guernsey's only significant industrial centre, St Sampson. The cranes and warehouses of the island's main cargo port and the power station's fuming chimneys don't often feature on Guernsey's picture postcards, but if you like ports or industrial archaeology, you may appreciate St Sampson's gritty authenticity. It also has some useful, reasonably priced shops, too.

For those who appreciate a look into a more distant past, several Neolithic sites have been discovered in nearby Vale, Guernsey's

🔺 *Loop-holed tower at L'Ancresse Common*

northernmost parish. Les Fouaillages (small burial chambers) were unearthed on the golf course on L'Ancresse Common in 1978. Amateur archaeologists may also like to track down the megalithic dolmens (passage graves) of Les Vardes and Dehus.

Tucked into a sheltered rock basin on the island's northeast tip is Beaucette Marina, full of classy-looking ocean-going yachts. If you enjoy walking, follow the coastal headlands – marvellous sites for migrant birds in spring and autumn. Castles and towers stud the headlands at every turn – Vale Castle, Rousse Tower and Fort Doyle are some of the most impressive. Large stretches of sand and reefs lie exposed at low tide, especially in L'Ancresse Bay or around Le Grand Havre. L'Ancresse Common is a gorse-covered stretch of moor and pastureland dotted with pine trees and placid tethered cattle. (See page 42 for further details on the beaches in the area.)

If you're feeling active, you might like to try the go-kart track just north of St Peter Port, or the windsurfing centres at Cobo and L'Ancresse bays. Fishing and diving expeditions can also be arranged. Swimmers should be careful on these coasts – even the sheltered eastern side has deceptively strong currents.

THINGS TO SEE & DO

Guernsey Freesia Centre

For an insight into Guernsey's blooming mail-order flower business, visit these fragrant glasshouses to watch planting, picking and packing.
ⓐ Route Carré, St Sampson ⓣ 01481 248185 ⓦ www.fletchers-freesias. co. uk ⓛ 09.00–17.00 daily

Oatlands Village

This former brickworks houses a complex of craft studios and gift shops: glassware, pottery, silverwork and knitwear are just some of the things on show. There is also now a crazy golf course.
ⓐ Les Gigands, St Sampson ⓣ 01481 249525 ⓛ 10.00–17.00 daily

TAKING A BREAK

Good daytime restaurants in northern Guernsey are thin on the
ground, although it isn't difficult to get a snack. You may prefer to
stock up with picnic provisions or fish and chips, and find a quiet
beach somewhere.

The Beach House £ A family restaurant and café with a traditional menu.
Food – including snacks and afternoon tea – is served throughout the
day, until early evening. Relax in the informal inside, or eat alfresco and
enjoy the panoramic views of the bay. ⓐ Pembroke Bay, L'Ancresse
ⓣ 01481 246494 ⓦ www.beachhouseguernsey.com ⓛ Hours vary
according to season

Fryer Tuck's Halfway Cafe £ More than just a fish and chip shop, this
unassuming seafront café offers sit-down meals with salmon and steaks
as well as traditional takeaways, all at rock-bottom prices.
ⓐ 1 Commercial Place, St Sampson ⓣ 01481 249448 ⓛ 06.30–14.15
Mon–Sat, 09.00–14.15 Sun ⓘ Licensed, with parking

Indian Cottage £–££ Excellent and authentic Indian food, offering good
value. ⓐ 4 Westerbrook, St Sampson ⓣ 01481 244820 ⓛ 12.00–14.00,
18.00–23.00 daily

The Courtyard Brasserie ££ Located at Oatlands, this à la carte restaurant
has a terrace overlooking the gardens. Dine in the large conservatory,
where teas and light lunches are available. The evening menu has
achieved special recognition on the island with many awards for
excellence. In addition, vegetarian dishes and a full children's menu are
available. ⓐ Oatlands Village, St Sampson ⓣ 01481 249525 ⓛ 12.00–14.30,
17.30–21.30 daily

Castel & St Saviour

The parishes of Castel (also known as Catel) and St Saviour are dominated by three glorious bays: Perelle Bay, Vazon Bay and Cobo Bay on the north coast, the latter seamlessly becoming Saline Bay. Each beach has its own distinctive characteristics. Perelle Bay is created within a dramatic show of rocks with natural headlands either side, while Vazon Bay is a massive stretch of beach – in fact, the deepest, if not the longest, expanse of sand on the island. Its width makes it a magnet for surfers and sand-racers. Cobo Bay, with sand dunes hugging its northern perimeter, is one of the prettiest bays on the island, its belt of sand broken only by reefs.

Inland of these three bays, you'll find rolling hills, sleepy lanes and quite a few nature reserves – the island of Guernsey is home to more than 450 flowering plants and many of these can be seen in the Castel and St Saviour parishes throughout the seasons. Don't miss the lovely stained-glass windows at St Saviour's parish church.

◒ *Sunset over the vast expanse of Vazon Bay*

⬤ Saumarez Park is Guernsey's largest public park

THINGS TO SEE & DO

Bruce Russell & Son: Gold, Silversmiths and Jewellers

Watch skilled craftsfolk hand-finishing the elegant range of jewellery
and artefacts on sale in these 16th-century showrooms. Ancillary
attractions include immaculate gardens and the Furze Oven café.

ⓐ Le Gron, St Saviour ⓣ 01481 264321 ⓛ 09.00–17.00 daily (summer);
closed Sun in winter

Saumarez Park & Folk Museum

Don't confuse this fine estate with St Martin's Sausmarez Manor,
owned by a separate (and differently spelt!) branch of the ancient
seigneurial family. Here, Guernsey's National Trust has set up a folk
museum, re-creating typical period interiors. There are also nature trails,
a children's playground, tearooms and a shop.

ⓐ Castel ⓣ 01481 255384 ⓛ 10.00–17.30 daily (Easter–Oct)
ⓘ Admission charge

Telephone Museum

A century of long-distance communications equipment is on display in
this small suburban house, once a telephone exchange.

ⓐ Cobo Road, Castel ⓣ 01481 726518 ⓦ www.museums.gov.gg
ⓛ 14.00–16.30 Wed & Thur (May–Aug), 14.00–16.30 Fri only (April &
Sept). Groups can arrange visits outside these hours
ⓘ Admission charge

TAKING A BREAK

As in St Sampson and Vale, the selection of restaurants is somewhat
limited. However, the following pubs and restaurants are worth a visit.

The Rockmount £ One of Guernsey's best pubs, serving high quality
bar food in view of the bay. ⓐ Cobo Bay, Castel ⓣ 01481 256757
ⓛ 10.00–00.30 daily (food served until 21.00)

Crabby Jacks £–££ Sit inside or out in this popular local bar and bistro with an extensive menu, serving unpretentious dishes, including seafood, pizza, salads, grills and burgers. They also have a takeaway service. ⓐ Vazon Bay, Castel ❶ 01481 257489 ⓦ www.crabbyjacksrestaurant.com ⏰ 10.00–00.30 daily (check out of season)

Cobo Bay Hotel ££ Ambitious combinations of sweet and savoury ingredients and lots of fresh fish are on the dinner menus in this agreeable seaside hotel. Very attentive service and a good-value table d'hôte. It now has a sun terrace for alfresco eating and drinking: a perfect place from which to watch the sunset. ⓐ Cobo Bay, Castel ❶ 01481 257102 ⓦ www.cobobayhotel.com ⏰ 19.00–21.30 Mon–Sat, 12.00–14.00 Sun

The Farmhouse ££ This appealing hotel, with several dining areas (including poolside in summer) is a good choice for lunch, dinner or afternoon tea. The lunch menu consists of simple dishes including sandwiches and salads; dinner is much more sophisticated. ⓐ Route des Bas Courtils, St Saviour ❶ 01481 264181 ⓦ www.thefarmhouse.gg

Fleur du Jardin ££ Under new management, this charming farmhouse inn has achieved an enviable reputation for its food. You'll find traditional bar food (including good sandwiches) and more interesting restaurant fare with fresh fish, game and roasts. There are plenty of tables outside on the terrace or in the garden. ⓐ King's Mills, Castel ❶ 01481 257996 ⏰ 12.00–14.00, 18.00–21.00 daily ❶ Reservations advised

Hougue du Pommier ££ Non-residents are welcome at this pleasant old farmhouse hotel near Cobo Bay, which features filling lunch or evening bar snacks, and a full à la carte menu in the restaurant. ⓐ La Route de la Hougue du Pommier, Castel ❶ 01481 256531 ⏰ 12.00–14.00, 18.30–21.00 daily; bar food not available Sun evenings

St Pierre du Bois & Torteval

Southwestern Guernsey and the parishes of St Pierre du Bois (known locally as St Peter or St Peter in the Wood) and Torteval have a strikingly varied shoreline. The west coast, scalloped into wide, low-lying bays of rock and sand, changes dramatically between high and low tide, when the reefs lie exposed. With mighty Atlantic breakers, the coastline is popular with expert surfers, but novice swimmers should take care.

Round the dramatic Pleinmont headland on the southwestern tip, the coast takes on a completely different character. Here, the shoreline is cliff-fringed and rocky, hiding tiny, tidal scraps of sand. The waterline can be difficult and dangerous to reach from the cliff-top footpaths: take a picnic and enjoy the breezy scenery and wild flowers.

Defensive structures line this daunting coast, from Martello towers to German gun emplacements. Most impressive is the gaunt tower in Pleinmont. Inland are the parishes of Torteval, St Peter in the Wood and St Saviour (see page 27), which are less developed than other parts of the

⬤ *Fort Grey on Rocquaine Bay houses a fascinating shipwreck museum*

island. Quiet farmland is interspersed with a web of tiny rural lanes where you can get thoroughly and enjoyably lost.

Be sure to drive carefully along the west coast road in rough weather when the tide is in. Alarmingly, the waves sometimes wash right over the sea walls. However, in fine weather, the western seafront can be magical, especially at sunset when the rocks turn extraordinary hues of pink and gold. Watch it from the fortified headlands, where parking places can be reached by quiet access tracks off the comparatively busy main road.

THINGS TO SEE & DO

Cliff walks

Guernsey's hilly south coast is the prettiest part of the island for walking. Footpaths lead all the way along the coast, past watchtowers, coves and headlands – it is free of traffic but accessible by lanes with parking places at various points. Cliffs may be unstable; don't stray from the marked paths. You can pick up a comprehensive guide (with maps) to coastal walks from the tourist office.

Coach House Gallery

Housed in sympathetically restored farm buildings, this light, airy gallery displays works by local artists, including crafts and original prints at a wide range of prices.

ⓐ Route du Longfrie, St Pierre du Bois ❶ 01481 265339
🕑 11.00–17.00 daily

Fort Grey

The stumpy, white Martello tower on Rocquaine Bay was built in 1804 to defend the island against the French. Known locally as the 'Cup and Saucer', it contains a fascinating Shipwreck Museum, showing the perils of Guernsey's reef-strewn west coast.

ⓐ Rocquaine Coast Road, St Pierre du Bois ❶ 01481 265036
🕑 10.00–16.30 daily (Apr–Oct) ❶ Admission charge

Lihou Island

The tiny, privately owned island of Lihou, off the L'Erée headland, makes an unusual walk at low tide. There is just one house and the remains of a Benedictine priory. Check tide tables carefully before you cross; the causeway is uncovered for only a few hours. Guided walks are available. ⓦ www.lihouisland.com

TAKING A BREAK

This part of the island has a good range of eating places, including some of Guernsey's best. Most are easy to find along the larger roads.

Longfrie Inn £ This family-oriented country inn has plenty of satisfying but inexpensive bar food, along with cheerful menus for children, a garden and a play area. ⓐ Rue de Longfrie, St Pierre du Bois ⓘ 01481 263107 ⓛ 12.00–21.00 Tues–Sun, closed Mon and Sun evenings

Imperial Hotel ££ Three bars, plus a patio and garden, offer a choice of places from which to enjoy some excellent cooking near a lovely stretch of coastline with cliff walks and beaches. Huge carvery on Sundays. ⓐ Torteval ⓘ 01481 264044 ⓛ 12.00–13.45, 18.00–20.45 daily

Taste of India ££ This traditional-looking cottage, known as Sunset Cottage, offers an exotic, Indian-inspired menu. No extra charge for technicolour sunsets or a stroll along the strand. ⓐ L'Erée, St Pierre du Bois ⓘ 01481 264516 ⓛ 12.00–13.30, 18.00–22.00 daily

RESORTS

Forest, St Martin & St Andrew

The main roads close to St Peter Port are built up and congested with a surprising amount of rush-hour commuter traffic, but brief detours down the quiet lanes of St Martin lead to the idyllic, unspoilt headlands of Icart and Jerbourg, where quiet sandy coves nestle beneath dramatic cliffs. Icart is the highest headland on Guernsey.

More sheltered than the west coast or northern beaches, these coves are ideal for swimming, though some involve a steep trek. The best way to see this part of the island is on foot; follow the waymarked coastal tracks that follow the coast or direct you inland to the St Andrew countryside. Alternatively, take a boat trip from St Peter Port Harbour on a fine day and view the south coast from the sea.

THINGS TO SEE & DO

Catherine Best Studio

One of Guernsey's most renowned jewellery designers has a studio showroom in a converted windmill. Original, handmade pieces using precious and semi-precious materials, in a wide range of traditional and modern designs.

ⓐ The Mill, Steam Mill Lanes, St Martin ❶ 01481 237771
Ⓦ www.catherinebest.com 🕐 09.00–17.30 Mon–Sat, 09.30–17.00 Sun

German Occupation Museum

An authentic display of World War II memorabilia is on display here, recalling Occupation days in Guernsey. The day-to-day trials of the islanders are brought vividly to life in wireless crystal sets, diaries, press cuttings and ration books. Visit the tearooms to try some wartime parsnip coffee – if you dare.

ⓐ Near Forest parish church (opposite the airport entrance turning)
❶ 01481 238205 Ⓦ www.occupied.guernsey.net 🕐 10.00–17.00 Tues–Sun, closed Mon; winter times vary ❶ Admission charge

◯ *The tunnels of the German Underground Hospital in St Andrew*

● *Shells decorate the Little Chapel, near Guernsey Clockmakers*

German Underground Hospital

This dank, rambling tunnel complex, dug by slave labour, is one of the most chilling reminders of the German Occupation period on any of the Channel Islands. Despite the effort expended in its construction, it was scarcely used as a hospital, and served mainly as an ammunition dump.
ⓐ La Vassalerie Road, St Andrew ☎ 01481 239100 ⏱ 10.00–12.00, 14.00–16.00 daily (June); until 16.30 (July & Aug); restricted hours in winter ❶ Admission charge

La Gran'mère du Chimquière

This ancient Bronze Age curiosity, whose name means 'the graveyard granny', stands by the gate of St Martin's parish church. A female figure carved in stone, she is believed to have magical powers and, even today, flower garlands and good-luck tokens are placed on her head, especially after wedding ceremonies.
ⓐ St Martin's Church

Guernsey Clockmakers & Little Chapel

See the amazing collection of barometers and timepieces, from longcase clocks to novelty watches, many made on the premises. Nearby stands the Little Chapel, claimed to be the world's smallest church at only 5 m (16 ft) long. Inspired by the grotto shrine at Lourdes, it is smothered with shells, pebbles and fragments of coloured china.
ⓐ Les Vauxbelets, St Andrew ☎ Clockmakers: 01481 236161; Chapel: 01481 237200 ⓦ www.thelittlechapel.org ⏱ Clockmakers: 09.00–17.00 Mon–Fri, 10.00–16.00 Sat, closed Sun ❶ Chapel freely accessible all year

Moulin Huet Pottery

A cottage workshop gallery hidden in a leafy lane leading to a pretty, south-coast cove. On a visit in 1882, the painter Renoir was inspired by this part of the island. Porcelain, stoneware, paintings and crafts on sale, or you can simply watch the pottery being made.
ⓐ Rue Moulin Huet, St Martin ☎ 01481 237201 ⏱ 09.00–16.00 Mon–Sat, 10.00–12.00 Sun (Easter to Christmas only)

Sausmarez Manor

This impressive stately home is occupied by one of the oldest and most distinguished families in the Channel Islands. Entertaining guided tours of the house highlight fine furnishings and ancestral anecdotes. Additional attractions include exotic woodland gardens, a miniature railway and a challenging pitch-and-putt course, plus a new sculpture trail.

ⓐ Sausmarez Road, St Martin ① 01481 235571 ⓦ www.sausmarez manor.co.uk 🕒 10.30 & 11.30 Mon–Thur, closed Fri–Sun (Easter–Oct), plus 14.00 (June–Sept); other attractions 10.00–17.00 ❶ Separate admission charges (grounds free)

TAKING A BREAK

Many of the most appealing restaurants in this part of the island are in beautifully located hotels.

The Auberge ££ One of Guernsey's best restaurants, complete with cliff-top views, a garden and a terrace. The menu caters for most tastes, with good fish and seafood, but plenty on offer for meat lovers. ⓐ Jerbourg Road, St Martin ① 01481 238485 ⓦ www.theauberge.gg 🕒 12.00–14.00 Mon–Sun, 18.45–21.00 Mon–Sat

La Barberie ££ A very good choice, serving top-quality seafood as well as tempting meat dishes. You can have a full meal in the evening or a snack by the pool or in the bar during the day. ⓐ Saints Road, St Martin ① 01481 235217 🕒 12.00–13.45, 18.00–21.30 daily

Bella Luce ££ Recently upgraded in terms of both food and décor, this long-established manor hotel in a rural setting is an island favourite. Bar meals and afternoon teas are served in the gardens on fine days, with traditional à la carte fare in the evenings. ⓐ La Fosse, St Martin ① 01481 238764 ⓦ www.bellalucehotel.com 🕒 12.00–14.00, 18.30–21.30 daily

 ◗ *The winding path of Le Coupée, Sark*

EXCURSIONS

Out & about

Bailiwick beach tour

Depending how you count them, the Bailiwick's islands have well over 30 separate beaches (Guernsey alone has 27). They vary from grand scalloped bays, on Guernsey's low-lying western and northern coasts, to sheltered coves set in deep green hills. Take your pick, but check the wind direction first. Huge tides make a great difference to the appearance of local beaches. If you plan to swim or venture into rock formations or across causeways, always check the tide tables. The list of beaches that follows reads clockwise from St Peter Port on Guernsey, with separate lists for Alderney, Herm and Sark.

GUERNSEY

Havelet Bay This popular town beach is where Victor Hugo took his daily dips when he lived in St Peter Port. A scenic setting of wooded cliffs and views of Castle Cornet add to its attractions. Seawater tidal pools at La Valette. The bay has easy access by car or bus, and there are cafés and toilets.

Soldier's Bay This is a rocky bay with no facilities. There is access via a cliff path, and views to Herm.

Fermain Bay This beautiful, sheltered cove is often pictured in brochures, showing its sand backed by pebbles at low tide. There is access by boat, bus or a cliff path, and it has very clean water, a café and toilets. Parking is virtually non-existent.

Petit Port Gorgeous, south-facing sandy cove, which is kept reasonably quiet by its challenging 270 access steps, but remains popular with locals. There are no facilities.

Moulin Huet Bay This beach captivated Renoir in the 1880s and has a lovely setting that includes caves. Parking is nearby, but some walking is necessary. See the **Moulin Huet Pottery** while you're here, which also has a good tearoom.

Saints Bay A peaceful bay, with snorkelling but no parking.

Petit Bot A large, picturesque cove, sheltered by a headland. There is access by bus or from a nearby car park – follow the stream down the lane. There is a café here. Beware of the adjacent cove (Le Portelet) – the exit is cut off at high tide. Several other difficult-to-reach coves can be glimpsed beneath the Icart peninsula.

South coast Between Petit Bot and Pleinmont Point there is no accessible sand, just a lovely stretch of cliffs hugged by a footpath. The scenery becomes steadily wilder towards the west, culminating in an Atlantic promontory, guarded by fortresses.

Portelet Bay This exposed, west-facing beach is a mix of rocks and sand, with a small harbour. Easy to reach by car or bus, with toilets, parking and refreshments. There is a good bar at the nearby Imperial Hotel.

Rocquaine Bay An extension of the wide sand-and-rock Portelet Bay, but separated from Portelet by Fort Grey, housing the **Shipwreck Museum**.

⏺ *Almost tropical, the beautiful Fermain Bay*

There is a crafts centre and café opposite. At the north end are Fort Saumarez and Lihou island (low-tide access only).

L'Erée This bay reveals a wide crescent of pale sand at high tide, and has good facilities and safe bathing. There is a pleasant Indian restaurant opposite, a craft shop and a café.

Perelle Bay Mostly rock here, but with attractive headlands to either side.

Vazon Bay This bay features a huge scoop of sand divided by reefs. Surfing and sand-racing take place here, and the gently shelving beach is safe for paddling in calm weather. Good sunsets and plenty of facilities. Visit Fort Hommet at the northern end.

Cobo/Saline Bay This bay consists of a sand belt broken up by reefs – it is scenic at low water and backed by dunes to the north. There are plenty of facilities: public transport, fish and chips, shops and hotels. At high tide, the sea often washes over the sea wall.

Port Soif A cosy, horseshoe-shaped bay with large rocks backed by dunes and rock pools at low tide. Sheltered sand, but dangerous low-tide currents at the mouth of the bay.

Portinfer A beach with soft white sand, dunes and rock pools.

Le Grand Havre/Ladies Bay A large, complex bay with white sand, rocks and dunes, and a small harbour. See the Rousse Tower while you're here. Easier to reach with a car; the buses follow the main road.

Pembroke/L'Ancresse Bay Very large, sheltered beach, with safe windsurfing and cafés. There is a common and golf course close by.

Bordeaux Harbour/Petils Bay Quiet, low-lying beaches with a fishing harbour and views of Herm, but some dangerous low-tide currents.

Beaucette Marina, with its stylish ocean-going yachts, is tucked into an old quarry in the northeastern tip. Vale Castle guards it to the south.

ALDERNEY
Braye Bay Protected from westerly gales, this is ideal for swimmers.

Corblets Bay The quiet bay is dominated by Fort Corblets and has safe bathing and good surf.

Longis Bay A sheltered stretch of sand on the eastern coast, popular with swimmers and families.

Saye Beach Pronounced 'Soy', a stunning stretch by the campsite. White sand and gentle sea: good for families.

HERM
Belvoir Bay An intimate, sandy cove, Belvoir Bay is good for relaxation, but take care, as it is renowned for its strong currents at low tide.

Shell Beach This beach is Herm's pride and joy. A magnificent stretch of sparkling quartz and shell fragments looks truly tropical on a fine day and is the perfect place for beachcombing, sunbathing and building sandcastles.

SARK
Derrible Bay A pretty bay that has sand only at low tide.

Dixcart Bay A safe, sandy and scenic bay, spanned by an arch of natural rock. A relaxing and fun visit.

Pôt Bay This bay is difficult to reach because of the rock formation, and only really accessible to adventurous explorers.

Venus Pool Situated on Little Sark, this bay has very deep water and is tidal, but very dramatic.

St Helier, Jersey

Jersey is only an hour away by ferry from St Peter Port, Guernsey, and is well worth a visit. The island has 12 parishes, most enjoying their own little bit of the dramatic coastline, and the main resort and the 'city' of Jersey is St Helier. St Helier's waterfront, formerly a dreary area of commercial wharfs and ferry terminals dominated by a power station, continues to undergo a massive refurbishment. There are many new public spaces, fountains and facilities being created. The attractive buildings housing the Occupation Tapestry and the Maritime Museum are a good start. Across the sweeping, sheltered bay of St Aubin is Elizabeth Castle, a Tudor fortress, romantically floodlit at night.

Liberation Square, focus of post-World War II jubilation (notice the bronze sculpture of flag-waving revellers), makes a natural starting point. Nearby is the colourful Steam Clock. In the streets behind you'll discover the town's true character – quaint old shopfronts and names in Norman French. Visit the delightful old market and historic Royal Square, where one of the Commonwealth's oldest parliaments sits. Though densely populated, St Helier has its quieter side. The immaculate gardens of Howard Davis Park offer a peaceful retreat from traffic fumes.

ⓘ The new Jersey Pass smart card is a good value way to see many of the island's top attractions (you can get passes for two, four or six days). Visit Ⓦ www.jerseypass.com for more details.

THINGS TO SEE & DO

Elizabeth Castle

The unmissable causeway fortress in St Aubin's Bay dates from the 1590s, and was named after Elizabeth I. It houses history exhibitions and the Royal Jersey Militia Museum. Access is on foot (low tide only) or by an amphibious vehicle dubbed the 'duck' (extra charge). Behind the castle is the Hermitage, a 12th-century chapel dedicated to St Helier, who was murdered by axe-wielding pirates. ⓐ St Aubin's Bay ⓣ 01534 723971

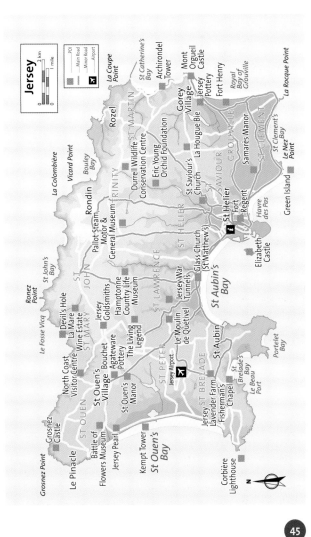

Jersey

0   1 mile
0   2 km

POI
Main Road
Minor Road
Airport

Grosnez Point
Le Pinacle
Grosnez Castle
Battle of Flowers Museum
Jersey Pearl
Kempt Tower
North Coast Visitor Centre
St Ouen's Village
St Ouen's Manor
St Ouen's Bay
ST OUEN
Le Fosse Vicq
Ronez Point
Devil's Hole
La Mare Wine Estate
ST MARY
Jersey Goldsmiths
Bouchet Agateware Pottery
The Living Legend
St John's Bay
ST JOHN
Hamptonne Country Life Museum
Pallot Steam, Motor & General Museum
Rondin
Bouley Bay
Vicard Point
La Colombière
TRINITY
Durrell Wildlife Conservation Centre
Rozel
ST MARTIN
La Coupe Point
St Catherine's Bay
Archirondel Tower
Mont Orgueil Castle
Jersey Pottery
Fort Henry
Gorey Village
Eric Young Orchid Foundation
La Hougue Bie
St Saviour's Church
ST SAVIOUR
GROUVILLE
Samarès Manor
ST CLEMENT
Le Nez Point
St Clement's Bay
Green Island
La Rocque Point
Royal Bay of Grouville
ST LAWRENCE
Jersey War Tunnels
Glass Church (St Matthew's)
St Helier
ST HELIER
Fort Regent
Havre des Pas
Elizabeth Castle
St Aubin's Bay
Le Moulin de Quétivel
ST PETER
Jersey Airport
St Aubin
ST BRELADE
Jersey Lavender Farm
Fisherman's Chapel
St Brelade's Bay
Le Beau Port
Portelet Bay
Corbière Lighthouse

N

🕐 10.00–18.00 daily (Apr–Oct) ❶ Admission charge. Access is difficult for disabled visitors

Fort Regent Leisure Centre

The curious golf-ball structure towering over St Helier's harbour houses a massive sports, leisure and entertainment complex in the grounds of a 19th-century fort. It has a 2,000-seater concert hall. Learn the history of the fort on a guided tour, and don't miss the signalling tower and the rampart views.

ⓐ Fort Regent ☎ 01534 449600 🕐 Opening times vary according to activity or event ❶ Admission free, pay as you play

Jersey Museum

An award-winning multimedia presentation of Jersey's history and culture, with an art gallery and excellent catering facilities. There are interesting sections on Lillie Langtry (Edward VII's glamorous mistress), and there is a restored merchant's house on the top floor.

ⓐ The Weighbridge ☎ 01534 633300 🕐 09.30–17.00 daily (summer); 10.00–16.00 daily (winter) ❶ Admission charge

Maritime Museum

In the same attractive, modern, waterfront premises as the Occupation Tapestry, this excellent museum has many entertaining 'hands-on' ways to learn about tides, winds, cleats and sails. A must for sailing enthusiasts.

ⓐ New North Quay ☎ 01534 811043 🕐 09.30–17.00 daily (summer); 10.00–16.00 daily (winter) ❶ Admission charge

Occupation Tapestry

An ambitious project, the Occupation Tapestry was completed in 1995 and involved the whole island. It contains over seven million stitches. The tapestry was made to commemorate the 50th anniversary of the Liberation, and each parish contributed one of the dozen panels depicting Jersey's wartime experiences. Housed in a quayside warehouse, there is an informative video and gift shop.

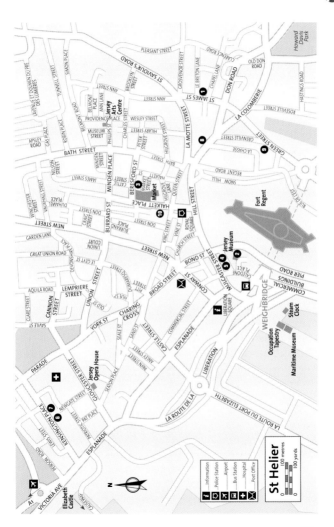

St Helier

0   100 metres
0   100 yards

- Information
- Police Station
- Airport
- Bus Station
- Hospital
- Post Office

ⓐ New North Quay **ⓣ** 01534 811043 **ⓛ** 09.30–17.00 daily (summer); 10.00–16.00 (winter) **ⓘ** Admission charge

TAKING A BREAK

As you might expect, St Helier has the widest choice of eating and drinking venues on the island, including chain restaurants such as Pizza Express and McDonald's. Several pubs offer regular live music in the evenings.

The Admiral Wine & Ale House £ **❶** One of St Helier's best-known haunts for inexpensive lunchtime food, decent bitter and dominoes. **ⓐ** 12–14 St James Street **ⓣ** 01534 730095 **ⓛ** 12.00–14.00, 18.00–20.15 Mon–Thur, 12.00–15.00 Fri–Sun

Jersey Museum Brasserie £ **❷** This excellent place is open to non-museum visitors and serves sophisticated snacks and cakes. **ⓐ** The Weighbridge **ⓣ** 01534 510069 **ⓛ** 12.00–15.00 daily, 18.30–21.30 Wed–Sat (Apr–Dec)

Atlantique Seafood Bar £–££ **❸** Located in the fish market in the centre of town, this is a must if you like fresh seafood. **ⓐ** Beresford Market **ⓣ** 01534 730033 **ⓛ** 09.00–15.00 Mon–Sat, closed Sun
A restaurant version of this popular place recently opened nearby. Unlike the original, it is open for dinner. **ⓐ** West Centre, Bath Street **ⓣ** 01534 720052 **ⓛ** 09.00–21.00 Mon–Sat, closed Sun

AFTER DARK

Despite its small size, Jersey has a wide range of entertainment. Much of it centres on St Helier, where pubs and clubs keep going until the small hours. In particular, the area surrounding the bus station is where many nightlife venues can be found. Check the *Jersey Evening Post* for the latest events. Nightlife tends to be busiest during the summer

⬤ *The striking bronze sculpture in Liberation Square*

St Helier's marina

months. You can choose from a band playing in Howard Davis Park to a rock band in Chambers pub (see below) or a jazz trio in the Blue Note Bar.

If your tastes are more highbrow, see what's on at the **Jersey Opera House** (ⓐ Gloucester Street ⓣ 01534 511115 ⓦ www.jerseyoperahouse.co.uk). This newly restored 600-seat theatre in Gloucester Street holds performances every week of touring musicals and plays. Also check out the **Jersey Arts Centre** (ⓐ Phillips Street ⓣ 01534 700444 ⓦ www.thisisjersey.com/jac), a smaller theatre hosting classical recitals, plays and art exhibitions. Jersey has two cinemas in town; the Odeon in Bath Street and Cineworld in the Waterfront Centre.

Outside St Helier, nightlife is rather quieter. At Wolf's Caves in St John, the Jersey Country Music Club meets weekly. If you want something different, you can join in with Latin, ballroom, sequence and Egyptian dance classes. Some hotels, including the Merton, provide entertainment open to non-residents.

Chambers £ ❹   A younger sibling of the long-established Admiral (see page 48), this popular pub appeals to a lively crowd, with regular music in the evenings. It has well-kept beers and serves good-value bar food. ⓐ Mulcaster Street ⓣ 01534 735405 ⓒ Food: 12.00–15.00 daily & 18.00–21.00 Mon–Thur

Café Zephyr ££ ❺   The café (there are also two other good restaurants) at the Royal Yacht Hotel is about the trendiest place to eat on the island. Contemporary food with Asian and Italian influences. ⓐ The Weighbridge ⓣ 01534 720571 ⓒ 09.00–22.00 daily

Candlelight Restaurant ££ ❻   This restaurant, which is part of a 17th-century coach house that is now the Revere Hotel, serves French and English cuisine in traditional surroundings. Fine wines are featured, and it is within walking distance of the Esplanade. ⓐ Kensington Place ⓣ 01534 611111 ⓒ 18.45–21.00 daily

Doran's Courtyard Bistro ££ ❼ An intimate ambience of warehouse windows, rustic beams and flagstone floors adds to the imaginative, eclectic fare served here. As to be expected, it is very popular with locals. ⓐ Kensington Place ☏ 01534 734866 🕓 18.00–21.45 Mon–Sat, closed Sun ❶ Reservation recommended

Olive Branch ££ ❽ An eclectic menu includes home-made pastas and the finest Italian sauces, while the good wine list has a plentiful variety of Italian wines. Light, modern décor and friendly staff. ⓐ 35–39 La Colomberie ☏ 01534 615993 🕓 12.00–14.00, 18.00–21.30 Mon–Sat, closed Sun

Bohemia ££–£££ ❾ The Club Hotel's restaurant has very quickly made a reputation for itself under talented chef Shaun Rankin, and is now one of the top couple of restaurants on Jersey. The ambience is sophisticated, and the food modern, using the highest quality ingredients. In the evenings, Rankin likes to produce dishes combining meat and seafood, but the lunchtime menu is simpler – and cheaper. ⓐ Green Street ☏ 01534 880588 ⓦ www.bohemiajersey.com 🕓 12.00–14.30, 19.00–22.00 Mon–Sat, closed Sun

La Capannina £££ ❿ An accomplished Italian restaurant, serving traditional cuisine using local produce. It also has a quality wine list. ⓐ 65–67 Halkett Place ☏ 01534 734602 🕓 12.00–14.00, 19.00–22.00 Mon–Sat, closed Sun

Southern tour, Jersey

St Peter is first landfall for most visitors to Jersey – the island's airport is here. St Brelade, in the southwestern corner, is one of the best known and best loved of Jersey's parishes. St Brelade's Bay is the island's most attractive beach resort, basking amid palm-fringed gardens. It boasts of being the most southerly seaside town in the British Isles – a claim occasionally challenged by St Helier.

Though somewhat suburban in parts, both parishes have surprising swathes of unspoilt greenery. **St Peter's Valley** is one of Jersey's prettiest and greenest drives. With two separate stretches of coastline, St Peter offers access to Jersey's largest beaches and a variety of watersports facilities. St Brelade's capitalises on one of Jersey's best family beaches. Glorious, peaceful coves nestle between rocky headlands to either side,

◆ *St Brelade's Bay*

and rare wildlife haunts the open spaces behind. Beyond the fortified promontory of Noirmont, St Aubin has a distinctive salty character and is home to the prestigious Royal Channel Island Yacht Club.

Next are the parishes of St Lawrence and St Saviour. You'll certainly find yourself travelling through these central parishes at some stage. They suffer rather from their proximity to St Helier, with busy traffic routes and built-up areas, but inland these are soon outstripped. St Lawrence has several interesting sights. The huge bay of St Aubin's is a fine, firm crescent of sand, if rather spoilt by the busy road running directly behind.

Two of the most interesting attractions in St Lawrence are the **Jersey War Tunnels** (see page 57), an amazing complex of underground tunnels constructed in the last war, and the **Hamptonne Country Life Museum**, run by the Jersey Heritage Trust and occupying one of the finest farmhouses in the parish. As you drive around, you'll see other impressive examples of Jersey's vernacular domestic architecture, too. Several of these buildings are looked after by the National Trust for Jersey (though not open to the public). Look out for Morel Farm and Le Rat Cottage.

A couple of churches are worth visiting, too: Millbrook's **Glass Church** (St Matthew's) is decorated with astonishing Lalique glasswork, like sculpted ice, while St Saviour's Church is the last resting place of the dashing Emilie Charlotte le Breton, better known as Lillie Langtry. Nearby, have a look at the imposing residence of the Lieutenant Governor, the Queen's representative on Jersey.

St Clement and Grouville are different again. Once free of St Helier's suburban tentacles, the hinterland of these southern parishes consists of open farmland and proper villages boasting rustic inns and churches. Take a drive along the coastal road past St Clement's Bay at low tide to see a strange lunar seascape of exposed reefs and rocks. It's particularly dramatic in morning light, so bring your camera. There are free parking places at intervals. Take care if you walk along the beach – the incoming tide moves extremely fast and can be dangerous.

THINGS TO SEE & DO

Fisherman's Chapel

The stippled frescoes in the early Norman chapel behind St Brelade's Bay look as though some agile leopard has had a shot at wall-painting with its paws.

ⓐ St Brelade's Bay ❶ Donations welcome

Glass Church (St Matthew's)

This intriguing church contains remarkable moulded white glass by the French glassmaker and jeweller René Lalique.

ⓐ Millbrook, St Lawrence, near Coronation Park ❶ 01534 720934
🕐 09.00–18.00 Sun–Fri, closed Sat (summer); 09.00–dusk Sun–Fri, closed Sat (winter) ❶ Donations welcome

Hamptonne Country Life Museum

An enjoyable folk museum comprising reconstructions of Jersey rural scenes, craft demonstrations, a nature trail and farm animals. Periodic special events.

ⓐ La Rue de la Patente, St Lawrence ❶ 01534 863955 🕐 10.00–17.00 daily (Apr–Oct) ❶ Admission charge

La Hougue Bie

Deep in rural seclusion stands a 12-m (40-ft) mound pierced by a mysterious passage entrance. It's a Neolithic burial site dating back more than 5,000 years. Later ages added medieval chapels and a German underground bunker. A visitor centre interprets the site simply and accessibly, paying particular attention to children.

ⓐ Route de la Hougue Bie, Grouville ❶ 01534 853823 🕐 10.00–17.00 daily (Mar–Oct) ❶ Admission charge

Jersey Goldsmiths

This widely promoted attraction is featured on many sightseeing tours. You can watch craftsmen at work and investigate a huge range of

◆ Visit Jersey Lavender Farm for the wonderful scents

costume jewellery, much of it plated in 18-carat gold. Repairs and adjustments are also carried out, and there is a terrace restaurant.
ⓐ Lion Park, in the heart of the island in the St Lawrence parish, Lion Park, St Lawrence ☎ 01534 482098 🕙 09.30–17.00 daily

Jersey Lavender Farm

Lavender is grown and harvested on the farm, and the oil is then extracted and blended into cosmetics and toiletries. Visit the farm, the café, the distillery and, of course, the shop. There is also a video presentation. A good time to visit is in June when the harvest begins.
ⓐ Rue du Pont Marquet, St Brelade ☎ 01534 742933 Ⓦ www.jersey lavender.co.uk 🕙 10.00–17.00 Tues–Sun, closed Mon (May–Sept)
ⓘ Admission charge

Jersey Pottery

This successful family-run pottery makes a thoroughly enjoyable excursion. Visitors may watch its charming, handmade ceramics being thrown, fired and painted by skilled artists. A showroom displays the results, and there's no pressure to buy. Other on-site attractions include the Glaze Craze, which allows you to have a go at painting your own design, and a good café and pub. The pottery stands in lovely gardens.
ⓐ Gorey Village ☎ 01534 851119 🕙 Showroom 09.00–17.30 Mon–Sat, 10.00–17.30 Sun; no production on Sat and Sun

Jersey War Tunnels

This graphic evocation of the Occupation period is set in a complex of tunnels dug by forced labour and equipped as a hospital for German casualties. It includes fascinating reconstructions and film footage.
ⓐ Meadowback, St Lawrence ☎ 01534 863442 🕙 10.00–18.00 daily (Mar–Nov); last admission 16.30 ⓘ Admission charge

The Living Legend

One of Jersey's foremost attractions, The Living Legend incorporates a multimedia presentation of the island's story (The Jersey Experience)

with lots of special effects. Standing within the same complex of landscaped grounds and play areas is adventure golf, a craft and shopping village, a restaurant, an ice-cream parlour and a fudge factory. ⓐ La Rue du Petit Aleval, St Peter ⓣ 01534 485496 ⓦ www.jerseysliving legend.co.je ◷ 09.30–17.00 daily (Apr–Oct); 09.00–17.00 Sat–Wed (Mar & Nov) ⓘ Admission charge

The entrance to La Hougue Bie, the Neolithic burial site (see page 55)

Le Moulin de Quétivel

See the mill wheel in action at this well-restored 18th-century watermill owned by the Jersey National Trust. There is also stoneground flour for sale, and a herb garden.

ⓐ Mont Fallu, St Peter ☎ 01534 745408 ⓦ www.nationaltrustjersey.org
🕙 10.00–16.00 Sat, closed Sun (May–Sept) ❶ Admission charge
(free to National Trust members)

Samarès Manor

This Norman seigneurial manor has a magnificent herb garden and plant nursery, as well as a good café. Guided tours of the house and the agricultural and carriage museum are available.

ⓐ Inner Road, St Clement ☎ 01534 870551 🕙 09.30–17.00 daily; tours of house Mon–Sat (additional charge); free garden talks Mon–Fri afternoons (Mar–Oct) ❶ Admission charge

TAKING A BREAK

Jersey's southern coast rejoices in several superb restaurants with moderate prices. It's worth working up an appetite if you're heading in this direction.

British Union £ This popular roadside pub serves simple bar food and offers pleasant service, a games room and a children's playhouse.
ⓐ Main Road, St Lawrence, in the centre of the island ☎ 01534 861070
🕙 12.00–14.00, 18.00–20.30 daily (closed Sun eve & Mon lunch)

The Hamptonne Café £ The Country Life Museum's attractive café will organise a picnic for you to eat in the meadow, or provide snacks and teas throughout the day. Typical Jersey recipes are served. ⓐ La Rue de la Patente, St Lawrence ☎ 01534 862698 🕙 10.00–17.00 daily (Apr–Oct)

Old Portelet Inn £ An excellent place for families, this dashingly converted farmhouse inn occupies a splendid location above Portelet

Bay. Great-value bar food and well-kept ales. Tables outside, music some evenings and friendly service. **ⓐ** Portelet, St Brelade **ⓣ** 01534 741899 **ⓛ** Tues–Sun lunch and evening meals, closed Mon

Pembroke £ This welcoming pub draws both visitors and locals for its friendly-family atmosphere and good-value food at lunchtime and in the evenings. **ⓐ** Grouville Coast Road, Grouville **ⓣ** 01534 855 756 **ⓛ** Food served 12.00–14.15, 18.00–20.15 daily

Smugglers Inn £ Down by the beach at Ouaisné, this traditional family pub serves wholesome lunches and dinners, popular after a day on the beach. **ⓐ** Ouaisné, St Brelade **ⓣ** 01534 741510 **ⓛ** 12.00–14.00, 18.00–21.00 daily, closed Sun evening in winter

The Victoria £ Popular family pub in the rural centre of the island. **ⓐ** St Peter's Valley **ⓣ** 01534 485498 **ⓛ** Lunch and dinner Tues–Sat, traditional roasts for Sun lunch, closed Mon

▲ *Old Portelet Inn, St Brelade*

Feast £–££ You can expect tasty, French-influenced food – such as moules, grilled garlic prawns and fish pie – at this newish place, with a welcoming interior and outside tables facing the harbour.
ⓐ 10–11 Gorey Pier **ⓣ** 01534 611118 **ⓦ** www.feast.je **ⓛ** 12.00–14.30, 18.00–23.00 Tues–Sun, closed Mon

Jersey Pottery Restaurants £–££ After much-deserved praise in several food guides, these two eateries are now just as popular as the pottery. The cooks use quality produce and local fish. Spinnakers Bar and Grill and the gastro bar, Castle Green, offer excellent value. **ⓐ** Gorey Village, Grouville **ⓣ** 01534 851119 **ⓛ** 09.00–17.30 daily, evenings in summer

Green Island ££ This low-key place occupies a prime location overlooking the dramatic reef-strewn coastline of St Clement's Bay. The simple interior and modest prices disguise some very interesting cooking (the owner is a celebrated Jersey restaurateur). There are also inexpensive takeaways and snacks. **ⓐ** Green Island, St Clement's Bay
ⓣ 01534 857787 **ⓛ** 12.00–14.30, 19.00–21.30 Tues–Sat, 12.00–14.30 Sun, closed Mon

Old Court House Inn ££ A fine, historic building on the harbour front, as popular for its characterful interior and friendly service as for its excellent food and ales. Several bars and dining rooms offer varied menus and ambience. You may remember it as a well-used backdrop to the 1980s TV series *Bergerac*. **ⓐ** St Aubin's Harbour, St Brelade
ⓣ 01534 746433 **ⓛ** 12.30–14.30, 19.00–22.00 daily

The Salty Dog Bar & Bistro ££ Concentrating on fusion food, with influences from around the world, but based on local ingredients. A local favourite. **ⓐ** Le Boulevard, St Aubin, St Brelade **ⓣ** 01534 742760
ⓛ 12.30–14.15 Fri–Sun, 18.00–21.30 Mon–Fri, 19.00–21.30 Sat

Tides ££ The popular restaurant at the Somerville Hotel, above St Aubin's Bay, serves sophisticated cuisine, as well as simpler dishes. Go at

lunchtime for the breathtaking views. ⓐ Mont du Boulevard, St Aubin
ⓣ 01534 741226 ⓛ 12.30–14.00, 19.00–21.00 daily

Village Bistro ££ An innovative menu that uses local produce to good
effect in appetising, modern dishes. Set menus represent excellent value.
ⓐ Gorey Village, Grouville ⓣ 01534 853429 ⓛ 12.15–14.00, 19.00–21.00
Tues–Sat, 12.15–14.00 Sun, closed Mon

Longueville Manor ££–£££ One of Jersey's most august and celebrated
restaurants, set in a country house hotel. Smart and formal but very
comfortable. Fine gastronomy menus using homegrown produce.
Vegetarian options. The set lunch is a bargain. ⓐ Longueville Road,
St Saviour ⓣ 01534 725501 ⓦ www.longuevillemanor.com
ⓛ 12.30–14.00, 19.00–22.00 daily

Ocean Restaurant ££–£££ If you want a special treat, head to the smart
restaurant at the swish Atlantic Hotel. On a good day, you can enjoy
great views, matched by Mark Jordan's acclaimed cooking – based on the
finest fresh local ingredients (they even have scallops specially caught by
a diver) and presented to the highest standards. ⓐ Le Mont de la
Pulente, St Brelade ⓣ 01534 744101 ⓛ 12.30–14.30, 19.00–22.00 daily

△ *The Victoria, in rural St Peter's Valley*

Northern tour, Jersey

The northern coast of Jersey is easily accessible from Guernsey. Cliff paths stretch along the scenic northern headlands through the parishes of St Mary and St John, offering beautiful but taxing walks. There isn't much sand between Bonne Nuit Bay and Grève de Lecq, but energetic walkers can explore many minor natural features, such as the Wolf's Caves or the Devil's Hole. Take care with cliffs and tides and watch out for warning signs.

This rugged coastline is best explored on foot, as the roads do not run by the sea. Some is National Trust land. A blaze of wild flowers can be seen in spring and summer and the area is a haunt of rare birds. It isn't always quiet, though: isolated headlands sometimes reverberate to the sounds of motorcycle scrambling or rifle shooting, and there are seasonal flickers of nightlife if you are out after hours at Grève de Lecq and Wolf's Caves.

There are a few small prehistoric sites, including tumuli, dating from around 3500 BC. L'Île Agois was once an islet hermitage, and can be reached at low tide. The hinterland is quiet and agricultural, scattered with fine examples of domestic architecture. For more information on this part of the island, it is a good idea to visit the North Coast Visitor Centre, housed in the Napoleonic-era barracks at Grève de Lecq.

You can have a closer look at some of Jersey's most traditional farmhouses by visiting tourist attractions such as La Mare Wine Estate or the Jersey Butterfly Farm. Another fine building called The Elms is headquarters of the Jersey National Trust. Most imposing of all is St John's Manor, a classically proportioned house open occasionally for charity events.

Jersey's northeastern parishes of Trinity and St Martin encompass the island's highest point, and some of its prettiest and most rural scenery. North of Gorey Village stretches a series of quiet, sandy bays, safe and unpolluted. Along the rugged northern shore, cliffs soar to a height of 120 m (400 ft) above the picturesque fishing harbours of Rozel and Bouley Bay. Inland, a spider's web of secretive country lanes conceals dignified, prosperous-looking farmsteads.

⬥ *Jersey's dramatic north coast: view towards Sorel*

One of these farmsteads, Les Augrès Manor, now hosts the world-famous zoo, set up by the late Gerald Durrell. Other popular sights in this part of Jersey include Mont Orgueil Castle in Gorey Village, and the exotic and riotously colourful blooms of the Eric Young Orchid Foundation. The massive breakwater at St Catherine's Bay also has a pier that is popular with anglers.

More ominous is the rocky outcrop called Geoffrey's Leap, where condemned criminals plunged to their enforced deaths in medieval times. The steep slopes behind Bouley Bay are the scene of an annual motorised hill-climbing championship.

The quiet reservoir of Queen's Valley, inland from Gorey Village , is also a nature reserve. The pathways leading round its edges make a gentle 1-km (½-mile) stroll. Take a picnic with you, or combine a walk with a visit to the nearby Jersey Pottery and its excellent brasserie/restaurant. There are additional car parks at either end of the reservoir.

THINGS TO SEE & DO

Durrell Wildlife Conservation Trust (Jersey Zoo)

The late Gerald Durrell's imaginative sanctuary and breeding centre has won many awards for its ground-breaking contribution to wildlife conservation. Rare species are rescued from the brink of extinction, and reintroduced to the wild. An informative, entertaining and inspiring place with a friendly, direct approach to visitors. A new meerkat enclosure was opened in 2009. The Café Dodo is a good bet for lunch or afternoon tea. 🅐 Les Augrès Manor, Trinity 🕿 01534 860000 🕘 09.30–18.00 daily (summer); 10.00–17.00 daily (winter) 🛈 Admission charge

Eric Young Orchid Foundation

Green-fingered visitors beat a path through tiny lanes to these exotic hothouses where the lifetime's work of an orchid addict can be seen. High summer is not the best time to visit, but there are gorgeous flowers all year round in an astonishing range of shapes and colours. A wonderful experience.

🔺 *Panoramic views from Mont Orgueil Castle*

ⓐ Victoria Village, Trinity ☎ 01534 861963 🕐 10.00–16.00 Wed–Sat, closed Sun ❶ Admission charge

Gorey Village

The picturesque cluster of harbour cottages dwarfed by Jersey's oldest castle makes a classic photo opportunity. Besides excellent restaurants, shops, local crafts and pubs, Gorey boasts several first-rate sights nearby and overlooks a magnificent beach. More good beaches and pretty countryside lie nearby. Needless to say, it's popular in high season, and parking can be difficult.

La Mare Wine Estate

These are Jersey's only commercial vineyards, planted in 1972 in the grounds of a fine 18th-century farmhouse. They produce in the region of 40,000 bottles of wine per season, along with their renowned cider and calvados apple brandy. La Mare also produces preserves, mustards, fudge,

traditional black butter and chocolates in its estate kitchens. There are videos and exhibitions, as well as tastings and produce on sale, an adventure playground for the children, and a good restaurant.
ⓐ St Mary ☎ 01534 481178 🕓 10.00–17.00 daily (Apr–Oct)
🛈 Admission charge

Mont Orgueil Castle
Recently restored, with many more areas open to the public, this splendid fortress, with lovely rampart views, has dominated Grouville Bay and Gorey Village since the 13th century, and is in remarkable condition. Exhibitions inside recount its history.
ⓐ Gorey, St Martin ☎ 01534 853292 🕓 10.00–18.00 daily (Mar–Oct); weekends only Nov–Feb 🛈 Admission charge

North Coast Visitor Centre (Grève de Lecq Barracks)
Housed in the neat, symmetrical buildings of a 19th-century Napoleonic-era barracks, this National Trust-owned visitor centre has displays and literature on local history, footpaths and wildlife.
ⓐ Grève de Lecq, St Mary ☎ 01534 483193 🕓 10.00–17.00 Wed–Sat, 13.00–17.00 Sun (May–Sept)

Pallot Steam, Motor & General Museum
Steam engines, farm machinery, theatre organs and other bygones, as well as occasional steam-train rides and special events.
ⓐ Rue de Bechet, Trinity ☎ 01534 865307 ⓦ www.pallotmuseum.co.uk
🕓 10.00–17.00 Mon–Sat, closed Sun (Apr–Oct) 🛈 Admission charge

TAKING A BREAK

There is some wonderful fine dining to be had along the north coast, along with good-value snacks in pubs and tearooms.

Les Fontaines Tavern £ Location is one of this old granite pub's selling points; it has spectacular ocean views. Inside, it has lots of character –

inglenooks, ships' timber beams and an ancient cider press. Randall's ales and inexpensive bar food served at lunchtime and dinner. ⓐ Route du Nord, St John ⓣ 01534 862707 ⓛ 11.00–23.00 daily

Gardener's Tearoom and Restaurant £ Good, wholesome family food served in the courtyard during the summer. Dishes such as local fish, pasta and exotic salads are prepared fresh on the premises. Delicious home-made cakes, bread and cream teas are also available. ⓐ Ransoms Garden Centre, La Grande Route de Faldouet, St Martin ⓣ 01534 853668 ⓛ Tues–Sun, closed Mon, lunch only

Royal St Martin £ Renowned for its excellent bar food, this landmark village pub in the centre of St Martin also has a separate restaurant. Good real ales. Families welcome. ⓐ Grande Route de Faldouet, St Martin ⓣ 01534 856289 ⓛ 12.00–14.15 daily, 18.00–20.30 Mon–Sat

St Mary's Country Inn £ One of the best examples of a Jersey speciality – the family-friendly country pub. Civilised and welcoming, this inn offers a hearty range of lunchtime and evening food. Family conservatory room and tables outside for alfresco summer dining. ⓐ Rue des Butttes, St Mary ⓣ 01534 482897 ⓛ 10.00–23.30 daily

The Seascale £ Simple, reliable pasta, pizza, sandwiches and Portuguese dishes. It also has outside tables. ⓐ Gorey Pier, Gorey ⓣ 01534 854395 ⓛ 09.00–21.00 daily (summer); 09.00–14.30, 17.30–22.00 daily (winter)

Rozel Bar and Restaurant £–££ This cosy pub serves much-acclaimed food, especially fish. Lunchtime fare is more traditional and less expensive, but the dinner menu is excellent. There are gardens and pub games available. ⓐ Rozel Bay, St Martin ⓣ 01534 869801 ⓛ Food served 12.00–14.15, 18.30–21.15 (except Sun evening in winter), closed Mon in winter ❶ Booking recommended in high season

Jersey's Green Lanes invite exploration

The Vineyard £–££ The restaurant attached to La Mare Wine Estate is pleasant for a snack, a light lunch or tea with home-baked cakes. Tables in the garden in fine weather. You may be able to taste some home produce here, including wine, cider or perhaps even calvados (apple brandy). ⓐ Rue de la Hougue Mauger, St Mary ⓣ 01534 484536 ⓛ 10.00–17.00 Mon–Sat, closed Sun (Apr–Oct)

The Bass & Lobster ££ Another welcome addition to Jersey's increasingly vibrant food scene. Local produce, with fish and seafood – as its name suggests – a speciality, served in a pleasant ambience. ⓐ Gorey Coast Road, St Martin ⓣ 01534 859590 ⓦ www.bassandlobster.com ⓛ Lunch 12.00–14.00 (Tues–Sat); dinner 18.00–21.00 (Mon–Thur), 18.00–21.30 (Fri–Sat), closed Sun

Suma's ££ This attractive venture offers discerning palates a chance to try first-class cooking at affordable prices. Under the same management as Longueville Manor (see page 62), Suma's has an airy upstairs dining room, simple but stylish, overlooking Gorey Harbour. Good-value set lunches. Children are welcome. It also features an in-house bakery and a good wine list. ⓐ Gorey Hill, St Martin ⓣ 01534 853291 ⓛ 12.00–14.15, 18.15–21.30 daily (closed mid-Dec–mid-Jan)

Château La Chaire £££ This luxury hotel-restaurant occupies a beautiful secluded spot near the island's northern tip. An elegant place, so book ahead and dress up. Cooking is ambitious 'modern British', and very fishy. The oak-panelled restaurant has a conservatory extension, and there's dining on the terrace in summer. ⓐ Rozel Bay, St Martin ⓣ 01534 863354 ⓦ www.chateau-la-chaire.co.uk ⓛ 12.00–14.00, 19.00–21.00 daily

St Ouen, Jersey

St Ouen (pronounced 'won') is Jersey's largest parish. It makes up the northwestern corner of the island, and is a varied and beautiful stretch of striking coastline and quiet farmland. Much is still uncultivated, making it a good place for walkers and nature lovers. Coastal paths follow most of the shore, partly on breezy cliff tops, partly beside peaceful dunes. There are some dangers on this exposed Atlantic seaboard, so it is wise to watch out for warning signs.

St Ouen boasts a large number of visitor attractions, although few merit more than a 'see if passing' rating. Many are clustered around L'Étacq and St Ouen's Bay, and most craft showrooms are free of charge. If you're keen on wildlife, visit the Kempt Tower and Francis Le Sueur Centre to learn more about Jersey's flora and fauna, or perhaps take in a guided nature walk through the reedbeds and lagoons behind St Ouen's Bay.

Grève de Lecq and Plémont Bay are two of Jersey's most appealing smaller beaches, while the giant, 8-km (5-mile) strand of St Ouen's Bay attracts surfers. Inland, the manor and church of St Ouen hark back to feudal times.

It's tempting to put your foot down if you are driving on the long straight road behind St Ouen's Bay. La Grande Route des Mielles is one of the few stretches on Jersey where this is possible. Be careful if you're walking across this road – especially with young children. If you are driving, remember the island's speed limit is only 65 kph (40 mph).

THINGS TO SEE & DO

Battle of Flowers Museum

A display of floats from Jersey's colourful annual parade, which usually takes place in August. Many of the award-winning floats were handmade by museum founder Florence Bechelet. Taped commentary is available.

ⓐ Mont des Corvées, St Ouen ☎ 01534 482408 🕐 10.00–17.00 daily (Easter–Oct) ⓘ Admission charge

● *Windsurfing at St Ouen's Bay*

Bouchet Agateware Pottery

A unique and secret process developed by founder Tony Bouchet lies behind the production of the stunning marbled ceramic pieces produced in this tiny pottery. Visit the showroom and find out more.

ⓐ Rue des Marettes, St Ouen ❶ 01534 482345 ⓛ 09.00–17.00 daily (limited opening times in winter)

Jersey Pearl

Simulated and cultured pearl jewellery is on show (and on sale) here, alongside other precious and semi-precious gems and watches. Find out what the largest pearl in the world looks like. There are workshop demonstrations and exhibitions as well as tea rooms and gift shops.

ⓐ North End Five Mile Road, St Ouen (also at Jersey airport and Gorey Pier shop) ❶ 01534 862137 ⓛ 09.30–17.30 daily (summer); 10.00–16.30 daily (winter)

Kempt Tower

The stumpy Martello tower at the north end of St Ouen's Bay houses a visitor centre and a video theatre dedicated to Jersey's natural history. Relevant literature is on sale. Nearby are the **Frances Le Sueur Centre** (another environmental information point) and **Les Mielles**, a nature reserve with beautiful sea views.

🅐 St Ouen's Bay 🕐 01534 483651 🕒 14.00–17.00 daily (May–Sept); free guided nature walks on Thur in summer ❶ Admission charge

Picnic spots

The cliff-top walk between Grève de Lecq and L'Étacq leads past some panoramic views. Plémont Point is a good spot for birdwatching: auks, fulmars and shags nest on the cliffs, while pipits and linnets flit across the open heathland behind. On a fine day, the 14th-century ruins of **Grosnez Castle**, 60 m (200 ft) above sea level, make a scenic vantage point. Further round the headland, **Le Pinacle** is a rock spire by the water's edge. A sea cave is exposed at low tide. Wild flowers carpet the treeless expanses of Les Landes in spring.

TAKING A BREAK

Colleen's Café £ A simple but good café. 🅐 Grève de Lecq Pier, St Ouen
🕐 01534 481420 🕒 08.30–17.00 daily

Moulin de Lecq £ The watermill theme of this delightful place makes it instantly appealing; you can see the machinery gears turning as you order drinks at the bar. Log fires, real ales and generous bar food add to its immense olde-worlde character. A children's playground and alfresco dining are available in the summer. 🅐 Grève de Lecq, St Ouen 🕐 01534 482818 🕒 12.00–14.00, 18.00–21.00 daily

Plémont Beach Café £ Only open during the day, but a reliable choice for a simple meal. 🅐 La Route de Plémont 🕐 01534 482005 🕒 09.00–17.00 daily (summer)

Alderney

Alderney, the most northerly of the Channel Islands, lies just 13 km (8 miles) west of Normandy's Cotentin peninsula. The island is only 2.5 km (1½ miles) wide and 5.5 km (3½ miles) long and is the perfect place to unwind, offering something for almost everyone.

It does not take long to get to Alderney (by plane) from Guernsey, or indeed to discover the attractions of its unspoilt open landscapes, wonderful cliff walks and beautiful, uncrowded beaches. Good leisure facilities and friendly pubs and restaurants add to the island's natural charms. At its heart lies the delightful town of St Anne, while Victorian and World War II fortresses stud the headlands. You can get free walking maps from the Visitor Centre in Victoria Street.

The island is home to numerous species of wildlife, flowers and marine life. There are two renowned nature reserves operated by the Wildlife Trust. **Longis Nature Reserve** is divided into 13 different habitats, from intertidal and coastal heathland to freshwater ponds, grasslands and woodland. Alderney's second reserve, **Val du Saou**, focuses on the island's only coastal woodland valley, where trees and birdlife thrive. It is also home to the leucistic (blonde) hedgehog.

Alderney was the first Channel Island to introduce duty-free goods. Alcohol and tobacco prices are certainly worth checking wherever you see the sign, but do your research first on other items. You may buy only if you are leaving the Bailiwick of Guernsey directly after your stay (in other words heading for Jersey or the UK).

BEACHES

Alderney has some good stretches of sand on its northern and southeastern shores, mostly fairly easy to reach. Some of the fastest tidal races in the world flow past the island. Cliffs make the southerly shore difficult to reach. The varied seabirds make Alderney's coastal walks interesting, but the many fortresses, some derelict, give it a forbidding air. Best for swimming and windsurfing is Braye Bay, protected from

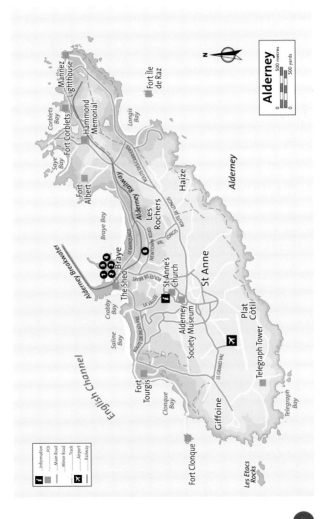

● *Sheltered Braye Bay is ideal for swimming and windsurfing*

westerly gales by the breakwater. Quieter Corblets Bay is dominated by
Fort Corblets and has safe bathing and good surf. Longis Bay – another
sheltered stretch of sand on the southeastern coast – is also popular.

THINGS TO SEE & DO

Alderney Breakwater
This huge Victorian granite structure, maintained by Guernsey, extends
over half a mile into the sea. Built as part of the UK's defence strategy,
and now essential to Alderney's economy (no seaborne freight could be
landed without it), it has inevitably suffered periodic storm damage and
its maintenance costs are phenomenal. After the Falklands War,
Guernsey agreed to pick up the tab for Alderney's breakwater as its
contribution to the British defence budget.

Alderney Railway
The Channel Islands' last remaining railway, built to carry granite
to the breakwater, offers 30-minute nostalgia rides in old London
Underground carriages in summer.

ⓐ Departs from Braye Road and Mannez Quarry ☎ 01481 822978
🕐 14.00–16.45 weekends and bank holidays (Easter–end Sept)
ⓘ Admission charge

Alderney Society Museum

Housed in an old school, this small collection traces the island's history from prehistoric times. The highlight is a group of artefacts – including a cannon – recovered from the wreck of an Elizabethan warship.
ⓐ Lower High Street, St Anne ☎ 01481 823222 ⓦ www.alderney society.org 🕐 10.00–12.00, 14.00–16.00 Mon–Fri, 10.00–12.00 Sat–Sun (Apr–Oct) ⓘ Admission charge

Boat trips

Trips on the *Voyager* or *Lady Maris* survey Alderney's coastal scenery or hop to France and the other Channel Islands. Seasonal and weather dependent.
ⓐ Information from the Alderney Visitor Information Centre, Victoria Street ☎ 01481 823737

Les Etacs Rocks

Alderney is home to one of the British Isles' rare gannet colonies, and here the birds sit beak to beak in a pungent top-dressing of guano. Nearby Burhou island is home to a small group of puffins.

Fort Clonque

One of Alderney's Victorian forts, which lies at the end of a concrete causeway. It is inaccessible at high tide (no admission inside fort).

Hammond Memorial

Plaques in several languages commemorate the Russian, Polish and Jewish slave-workers who perished under German Occupation while constructing Hitler's Atlantic Wall.

🔺 *In a spectacular setting, Fort Clonque is cut off from the mainland at high tide*

Mannez Lighthouse

Dating from 1912, the Mannez Lighthouse offers spectacular views of the razor-sharp reefs on this dangerous coast.

🅐 Quesnard 🕿 01481 823077 🕐 Guided visits weekends end May–end Sept.

St Anne's Church

One of the finest Channel Island churches, built of Caen stone and restored after wartime damage.

🅐 St Anne

Telegraph Tower

The high cliffs near this 19th-century signalling tower offer views of all the Channel Islands.

TAKING A BREAK

Alderney offers good eating and drinking places, nearly all of them clustered in St Anne or Braye Bay. Prices are slightly higher than on the other islands, due to freight costs, but licensing hours are more lenient; pubs stay open all day and every day, including Sunday. Seafood lovers should not miss the Seafood Festival in May.

Braye Chippy £ ❶   With a view of the harbour from the terrace, there is much more than fish and chips on offer here. You can take away, or bring a bottle (they don't have a licence) and eat there. ⓐ Braye Harbour ⓣ 01481 823475 ⓛ Closed Tues out of season

The Moorings £ ❷   Traditional, good-value bar meals, à la carte menu with great seafood and alfresco dining around the BBQ in summer. ⓐ Braye Street ⓣ 01481 822421 ⓛ 12.00–14.00, 18.00–20.30 Tues–Sun, closed Mon (autumn & winter)

Braye Beach Hotel ££ ❸   The island's newest and smartest hotel (it even has a fully equipped cinema) serves drinks, bar snacks and an impressive range of à la carte dishes. You can eat in the stylish dining room, or on the terrace – both with excellent views of Braye Bay. The set lunch menu is good value. ⓐ Braye Street ⓣ 01481 824300 ⓦ www.brayebeach.com

Bumps Eating House ££ ❹   Charming atmosphere with an impressive menu featuring international cuisine and an extensive wine list. ⓐ Braye Street ⓣ 01481 823197 ⓛ 18.00–23.00 Thur–Sat and Sun lunch, closed Wed

⬤ *The restored interior of St Anne's Church*

First and Last ££ ❺ Primarily a seafood restaurant, serving mouthwatering food that appeals to the eyes as well as the taste buds. ⓐ Braye Street ⓣ 01481 823162 ⓘ Closed end Sept–Easter

Harbour Lights Hotel ££ ❻ Recently restored, and under new ownership, the Harbour Lights has pleasant rooms, many with sea views. Eat or drink in the bar/restaurant, or on its array of terraces. The food is simple but impeccably cooked by one of Alderney's best chefs. ⓐ Newtown Road ⓣ 01481 823233 ⓦ www.harbourlightsalderney.com

AFTER DARK

Only the larger islands offer anything significant in the way of nightlife, and evening entertainment on Alderney is more likely to involve a jigsaw puzzle, a game of Scrabble® or a good book than a night on the tiles. Most hotels provide books and board games for evenings and wet days, and impromptu events, such as quiz nights or live music, may occasionally take place in local pubs. Alderney's evening entertainment mostly centres on pubs and restaurants. Visitors are welcome to join in local island happenings – talks, slide shows, whist drives, etc. You can generally find a game of whist, dominoes or bridge, or a darts match going on somewhere, and there's a tiny cinema in Victoria Street.

Herm

Tiny Herm – a mere 20-minute ferry-hop from Guernsey's St Peter Port – makes a marvellous outing for a fine day. With no cars (though you will see quad bikes and tractors) or organised attractions, Herm offers a deceptively simple but captivating mix of beautiful scenery, idyllic beaches and an irresistible invitation to relax and unwind. The island was quarried for granite in the 18th century, and was occupied by the Germans during World War II. One of its more famous residents was the novelist Sir Compton Mackenzie.

The island is just 2.5 km (1½ miles) long and 1 km (⅔ mile) wide, and you can walk round it in under two hours. Near the harbour stands a spotless Mediterranean-style 'village', colourwashed in ice-cream pastels, consisting of a hotel, pubs and a handful of little shops. Here, you can have a drink, a snack or an excellent meal. If you want to stay a little longer, the island also has holiday cottages and campsites.

⬤ *Remains of a Neolithic dolmen on Herm*

Central paths take you through woods and fields, past the castellated manor and a tiny medieval chapel. A herd of beef cattle grazes in the surrounding farmland.

If you strike south, you climb along cliff paths overlooking rocks and reefs, and the privately owned neighbouring island of Jethou (not accessible to visitors). The low-lying northern routes lead over heathland fringed by glorious belts of sand. Everywhere on Herm, wildlife flourishes among hosts of seabirds, clouds of butterflies and riotous flowers, while farm gates, fences, beach cafés and holiday cottages are kept in top order. The island also attracts many anglers.

The early morning 'milk boat' ferry offers a reduced day return to Herm from Guernsey – and a longer stay on the island. A couple of the afternoon sailings in summer, when the ferry runs more frequently, are also cheaper. Remember to check the weather forecast, as you'll be outdoors for much of the time.

HERM'S TENANTS

In 1949, Major Peter Wood and his wife, Jenny, took over a long lease on the island from the States of Guernsey, living at the Manor. Their enthusiastic enterprise and hard work resulted in today's civilised miniature paradise. Financed by farming and tourism, Herm continued to be managed by members of the Wood family (Jenny died in 1991 and the major in 1998), daughter Pennie, and her husband, Adrian Heyworth, until late 2008, when the remaining 40-year lease was bought by Guernsey couple John and Julia Singer for – it is rumoured – considerably less than the asking price of £15 million. The Singers have pledged to keep the island as it was. The resident population of 50 is doubled in summer by seasonal staff. Local children are educated in the tiny island school. Herm also generates its own electricity and has its own water supply and drainage systems.

BEACHES

Herm's pride and joy is Shell Beach, on the northeastern shore. This magnificent stretch of sparkling quartz and shell fragments looks truly tropical on a fine day and is the perfect place for beachcombing, sunbathing and sandcastles. There is also a small café. Rock pools trap

⬤ *Belvoir Bay, with Shell Beach beyond*

fascinating pockets of sealife at low tide, and the clear, gently shelving water is ideal for snorkelling. As the name suggests, the sand consists of millions of sparkling shells, whole or fragmented – some are thought to have been carried from the tropics on the Gulf Stream, though they could also come from deep local waters.

Herm's northern coast is an almost continuous belt of sand and dunes at low tide, easily reached if you're prepared to walk. Near the harbour the shoreline is muddier and rockier, good for messing about with a shrimping net. Belvoir Bay is a more intimate sandy cove further south (beware strong currents at low tide) with a café and toilets.

THINGS TO SEE & DO

Le Manoir

Herm's real 'village' centres round the imposing 15th-century manor, now the residence of the Heyworth family. The medieval-looking 'keep' is only a century old. Near the manor house are the island's power station, workshops and unobtrusive modern farm buildings.

Neolithic dolmens

In ancient times, Herm served as a sacred burial ground. Traces of several stone tombs remain in the north of the island.

La Pierre aux Rats

A large, prehistoric standing stone served as a seamark for centuries, until quarrymen removed it in the 19th century, thinking it was just another useful lump of granite. Local sailors protested strenuously, and the present obelisk was put back in its original place.

St Tugual's Chapel

This quaint little building dates from the 11th century, and its unusual bell tower remains its most striking feature. The chapel also contains attractive stained glass. Informal services are held every Sunday during the summer.

TAKING A BREAK

Herm operates seasonally, and in the winter the island's pubs and cafés may be closed. Check facilities before you sail. There is a small grocery shop open during the season, but you can always take a picnic.

The Mermaid Tavern £ ❶ The 'village inn', with good snacks, and full lunchtime and evening meals most of the year (and Sunday lunch in winter). With tables outside, and roaring fires in chilly weather. The brasserie (open in the evening) serves meat cooked on hot rocks.
☎ 01481 750050 🕐 12.00–14.30, 18.00–20.00 daily (summer), closed Mon & Thur (winter)

The Ship Inn ££ ❷ This pleasant pub-restaurant is part of the White House hotel (see below), offering lunchtime fare and more elaborate evening meals at the Captain's Table. ☎ 01481 750075 🕐 12.00–14.30, 19.00–21.00 daily (Apr–Oct)

The White House £££ ❸ Herm's only hotel caters primarily for resident guests but, space permitting, day visitors may book ahead for a table, for dinner only (smart dress requested). Light lunches are served in the hotel's lounges and gardens. Hotel rooms have no telephone or TV.
☎ 01481 750075 🌐 www.herm.com 🕐 12.30–13.30, 19.00–21.00 daily (Apr–Oct)

AFTER DARK

If sea air, good food and exercise don't suggest an early night, you may find yourself practising the age-old but much-neglected art of conversation. There are, however, occasional beach barbecues. To encourage social interaction, television is deliberately banished from Herm's White House hotel.

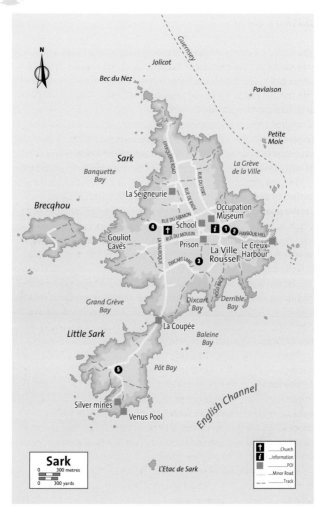

Sark

Situated less than 9.5 km (6 miles) east of Guernsey, Sark was a quaint political fossil – a last vestige of European feudalism – until late 2008, when its first democratic elections were held, voting 28 representatives into the Chief Pleas (Sark's parliament). Less than 5 sq km (2 sq miles) in area, Sark is home to about 650 permanent residents, but welcomes over a hundred times as many visitors every year. Five hours or so between ferry rides is short shrift to give this pretty place. Stay longer if you can – especially in spring, when Sark is carpeted with over 600 species of wild flowers.

Sark is a jagged rock plateau perching on 90-m (300-ft)-high cliffs, gashed by deep valleys leading to the sea. It is almost two islands, for the smaller southerly island, called Little Sark, is only attached to its big sister by a knife-edge ridge called La Coupée. Sark's scenery and individuality attract enough day-trippers to cause bicycle jams in high season. But if you stray off the beaten tracks, you will find secret coves and crevices all to yourself.

Like its close neighbour, Herm, Sark allows no visiting motor vehicles, and access to the island is by ferry only (though helicopters may land in medical emergencies). A tractor-bus service saves ferry passengers the 800-m (½-mile) climb up and down Harbour Hill. At the top of the hill lies a village of Toytown proportions.

The island's famous Dame Sibyl Hathaway, remembered for her courage during the German Occupation, was succeeded as Seigneur of Sark by her grandson, whose residence, La Seigneurie, is Sark's most impressive building. The Seigneur still holds a few privileges first granted by Elizabeth I in 1565. He is the only Sark-dweller permitted to keep doves, for example, or an unspayed bitch. More lucratively, until recently, he was entitled to receive one-thirteenth (Le Trezième) of the value of any Sark property that changed hands.

You can get to Sark all year round from St Peter Port, Guernsey, by ferry in around an hour, though note that ferry times and frequencies vary according to the time of year.

Democracy apart, things are set to change further on the island. The billionaire Barclay brothers, who live on neighbouring Brecqhou (and who helped to drive the constitutional change), now own several hotels and other businesses and property on Sark. Their investment may be a good thing, but nobody can be quite sure how it will all work out for the style of life on the island.

BEACHES

Access to most of Sark's cliff-backed coves involves a steep climb. Easiest to reach (from Dixcart Hotel) is **Dixcart Bay** – safe, sandy and scenic, spanned by an arch of natural rock. Neighbouring **Derrible Bay** has sand only at low tide. Adventurous explorers may discover **Pôt Bay** or the deep tidal **Venus Pool** on Little Sark.

THINGS TO SEE & DO

Boat trips

If you're only on Sark for a day, a boat trip is a bit ambitious, but in calm weather it's an enjoyable way to see Sark's intricate, cave-pocked cliffs, study the wide variety of seabirds and take in the salty air. Contact Sark Tourist Information Office for more detailed information on how to arrange a trip.
ⓐ The Visitor Centre, Harbour Hill ⓣ 01481 832345

Carriage rides

See Sark the leisurely way – by horsepower. Patient carthorses await the ferries in summer. You can pre-book a jaunt from Guernsey, or arrange your ride on arrival for a 90-minute or 2-hour excursion.
ⓘ 07781 113386/01481 832135, or contact the Tourist Office

La Coupée

This breathtaking neck of rock, linking Little Sark to the main island, was fenced by prisoners-of-war, and is just wide enough for a tractor or a horse-drawn carriage to pass across, with dizzying drops to either side.

Le Creux Harbour

Tunnels lead to this pretty, rock-walled harbour from the more modern and practical landing stage at La Maseline.

Occupation Museum

This museum highlights aspects of island life under the Germans during World War II, including photographs of the redoubtable Dame of Sark dealing with her uninvited guests. Sark escaped fairly lightly, with no serious food shortages and no fortifications.

❶ 01481 832564 ❷ 11.00–13.00, 14.00–16.00 daily (Easter–Sept)
❶ Admission charge

Prison

Sark's curious little jail stands in the village. It has just two cells, and is still occasionally used to detain miscreants before dispatching them to Guernsey for trial.

▲ *Beneath La Coupée lies Grand Grève Bay*

La Seigneurie

You can't look around the Seigneur's granite manor house, but his varied, beautiful gardens are open to the public and well worth seeing, with their roses, tender plants, a hedge maze and a Victorian greenhouse. Look out for the strange Gothic colombier (dovecote) and the antique cannon. You can take a break in the aptly named Hathaways Café.

📞 01481 832345 🕐 10.00–17.00 Mon–Fri (Easter–Oct), daily (July–Aug) ❗ Admission charge

Silver mines

The shafts and ventilation chimneys of Sark's 19th-century mining days can still be seen on Little Sark. The mines were never profitable, and were abandoned after a tragedy in 1845. Note that the mine site is privately owned, and that it is dangerous to explore it.

🔺 *The beautiful gardens at La Seigneurie*

◒ *Brecqhou – a very private island*

AN ISLAND OF YOUR OWN

'So, you like my island, Mr Bond ...' A separate island, Brecqhou, lies a stone's throw off Sark's northern tip. This was privately purchased in 1993 by the wealthy Barclay brothers – twin businessmen (owners of the *Daily Telegraph* and the Ritz hotel in London) whose reclusive entrepreneurial activities cause much local gossip. The move to democracy was partly forced by the Barclays, who were disappointed, to put it mildly, when few of their supporters got elected. Passing ferries give a tantalising glimpse of a huge, newly built Gothic castle rising from Brecqhou. This extraordinary lair was constructed by a Guernsey workforce sworn to secrecy. Rumours of nuclear bunkers, summit conferences and private casinos flourish, fuelled by vigorous denials and determined resistance to trespassing.

TAKING A BREAK

Sark's most sophisticated eateries are its hotel-restaurants. Choice is restricted in winter when most hotels close. You can buy picnic provisions and cakes at the village's Island Stores.

Stumbles £–££ ❶ This is one of the few places open in winter (when takeaways are also available). Have a drink in the bar, or eat in the attractive conservatory or the garden. Portions are big and the menu tempting. ⓐ Rue Lucas ❶ 01481 832302 ⓛ 12.00–14.00, 18.30–21.30 Mon–Sat, closed Sun (summer); Wed–Sat & Sun lunch, closed Mon & Tues (winter)

Aval du Creux Hotel ££ ❷ Simple lunches, cream teas and dinner in a pleasant setting, with tables outside. ⓐ Next to the Tourist Office ❶ 01481 832036 ⓦ www.avalducreux.co.uk ⓛ 11.00–17.30 daily

Dixcart Hotel ££ ❸ One of Sark's oldest and most respected hotels (pronounced 'dee-cart') welcomes non-residents with a tasty range of snacks and meals, including a children's menu and seafood specials. ⓐ Dixcart Valley ❶ 01481 832015 ⓦ www.dixcartbayhotel.com ⓛ All year

Hotel Petit Champ ££ ❹ A west-coast setting with sea views accompanies everything, whether you're enjoying sandwiches or a candlelit dinner. Serves lobster and crab. Sheltered garden. ⓐ On the west coast; from the Methodist Chapel, follow hotel signs ❶ 01481 832046 ⓦ www.hotelpetitchamp.co.uk ⓛ All year

La Sablonnerie Hotel ££ ❺ This acclaimed farmhouse hotel serves fresh fish and home-grown produce, Sark cream teas and seafood platters. ⓐ Little Sark ❶ 01481 832061 ⓦ www.lasablonnerie.com ⓛ 12.00–14.30, 19.00–21.00 daily (Easter–Oct)

◗ *Enjoy Guernsey's country lanes and hidden secrets*

LIFESTYLE
Island life

Food & drink

Unlike the unfortunate islanders who endured wartime occupation on grisly fare like parsnip coffee and peapod tea, today's holidaymakers can expect good rations. Eating is an important part of life in Guernsey and its islands. Local ingredients, especially seafood, market garden vegetables and dairy produce, are renowned for their freshness and quality. But many staples have to be imported, so the cost of eating out, or shopping for self-catering, may be higher than you expect.

Excellent and imaginative cooking can still be had at moderate prices in Guernsey, with many tourist restaurants and beach cafés, remaining heartily traditional. Whatever the map suggests, the majority of culinary styles are closer to England than to France. Croissants and baguettes are on sale in the bakeries, but you're more likely to find a classic British fry-up on your hotel breakfast plate. At Sunday lunchtimes, traditional

THE ORMER

The mysterious ormer (more widely known as abalone), a large mollusc that looks like an asymmetrical limpet, derives its name from the French *oreille de mer* (sea ear).

The Channel Islands are the northern limit of its habitat, yet this local delicacy is now rare due to over-fishing. As such, strict regulations apply to the collection of ormers. They must only be harvested between the months of September and April, and only on the first day of the full moon and for the three days after. During this period, Jersey men and women scour the rocks to find the sought-after ormer. These rules are strictly policed and heavy fines are levied on offenders.

Once found, the ormer is prised from the underside of rocks by hand and carried to shore in a traditional ormer basket. It is then beaten and cooked in the oven as a casserole or served with gravy, carrots and onions. The ormer's striking mother-of-pearl inner shell is also used as decoration on houses and for jewellery.

SMOKING

Smoking in enclosed public areas and workplaces is not permitted in Guernsey and Herm. This includes pubs, restaurants, hotels and guest accommodation. There is an exception permitting smoking in designated guest bedrooms, but such rooms are few in number so please check before you book. Alderney has similar legislation with no smoking in hotel bedrooms. Sark does not currently have legislation, although the majority of businesses operate a voluntary ban.

carvery roasts are always popular. Dozens of friendly, family-oriented pubs offer well-tried favourites like ploughman's lunches and chilli con carne, though these aren't the only things on bar menus. There's no shortage of cafés for cream teas, fish-and-chip shops for filling takeaways, and Indian, Chinese or Italian restaurants to provide reliable, inexpensive solutions to hunger pangs. There are also an increasing number of restaurants that are reaching culinary heights, strongly influenced by French cuisine.

All kinds of cakes and scones appear in the islands' tea gardens and coffee shops. For something local, look out for *fiottes* (balls of sweet pastry) and Guernsey *gâche* (pronounced 'gosh'), which is a fruit tea bread. You can sometimes buy this ready buttered by the slice. Look out for Jersey Wonders (a kind of doughnut) and don't forget to try some Channel Island fudge; it's available in an amazing range of flavours.

Most people are aware of Channel Island 'gold top' milk, with its high butterfat content. Butter and cream are produced in huge quantities, enriching local menus everywhere. Apart from a little Guernsey cheddar, you won't see much island-produced cheese – the milk sours too quickly. Herm has its own richly yellow ice cream, not available elsewhere.

Huge swathes of Guernsey are under glass, which produces some wonderful fruit and vegetables, although crops have altered in line with commercial pressures. Tomatoes, ousted by subsidised foreign

◓ There is plenty of local seafood on the menu

competition, have often given way to flowers. Market gardening is still important, however. Jersey Royal new potatoes, boiled and buttered with herbs, are certainly a dish fit for a queen or a king.

Strawberries, celery, courgettes and many salad crops are raised for local consumption as well as the export trade. You'll often see produce on sale in little hatches by the roadsides, accompanied by an honesty box to leave money in.

Finned or shelled, fish dishes feature on nearly every island menu. In the fast, tidal waters surrounding the Channel Islands, pollution levels are much lower than in some holiday destinations, so eating shellfish is less like playing Russian roulette with your stomach. Besides crab, brill and sea bass, look out for Sark lobster. In the Channel Islands, humble British fish and chips attains classic status, but you will also find more elaborate French-style dishes like those popular in nearby Brittany and Normandy. Conger eel soup is a local favourite. Some expensive kinds of seafood, such as spider crab and lobster, are sold by weight rather than by portion. Check carefully when you order, to avoid a nasty shock when you receive the bill.

One country recipe widely promoted as an island classic is the bean crock, or bean jar – a ribsticking casserole of pork, beans and onions. You may also come across black butter, which, despite its name, contains no dairy products at all. Instead, it's a long-brewed mixture of apples, sugar, lemons and cider, flavoured with liquorice. Try it spread on a slice of *gâche* (see page 97).

The Normans introduced cider to the islands (look out for Rocquettes), but today beer is more popular. The Channel Islands also produce their own version of a cream liqueur, rather like Baileys. You may find an apple brandy on Jersey, made at La Mare Wine Estate. Local beers you are likely to see everywhere include Guernsey Brewery ales and Mary Ann from Jersey. Randalls no longer brews its own beer, but imports real ale and owns many Channel Island pubs. You can find excellent pubs all over the islands. On Alderney, if you're there for Milk-o-Punch Sunday in May, you'll be offered the punch (consisting of milk, eggs, rum, nutmeg and sugar) throughout the island.

Shopping

The Channel Islands market themselves as an inexpensive destination because duties are low and there is no VAT. Freight costs can erode this advantage and you should take advice before arranging for purchases to be shipped directly to the UK – you may end up having to pay VAT when they pass through customs. Also, don't forget that non-EU customs restrictions apply to any luxury purchased in the Channel Islands that you take back to the UK. Alcohol and tobacco are relatively cheap, but savings on other goods are not always as great as you might expect. Prices vary significantly from one outlet to another, and from island to island, so shop around.

St Peter Port (see pages 18–23) has the best shopping centres and streets in Guernsey. The High Street in St Peter Port, and the old market (now a shopping centre) are good places to head for, and the streets around Victoria Road also make a good starting point for a shopping spree.

ISLAND CRAFTS

For a one-stop centre where you can do all your souvenir-buying in one go, your best bet is to head for Guernsey's Oatlands Village in St Sampson, in the north, where you can watch local craftspeople at work at a number of different traditional industries.

JEWELLERY

Some of the largest jewellery showrooms on Guernsey are in St Peter Port. Look out for 'ormer shell' jewellery and items made from tiny spoons or Guernsey milkcans. Check the workshops of Catherine Best (the Old Mill, St Martin), a leading designer of modern jewellery, and Bruce Russell (Le Gron, St Saviour). Also head for the Oatlands Craft Centre, in St Sampson. Note that Channel Island gold and silver is not subject to the same rigorous assay and hallmarking process as it is in the UK. Any 'guarantee' offered with jewellery generally refers to the quality of workmanship, rather than any intrinsic value.

● *Enter a time warp at the National Trust's Victorian Shop*

KNITWEAR

A real Channel Island sweater makes an excellent buy. A classic Guernsey is instantly recognisable. The oiled wool is specially stitched, twisted and seamed to repel water.

Traditional, hand-finished Guernseys are produced at Le Tricoteur, which has a factory shop at Perelle Bay and a retail outlet in St Peter Port. For a sweater with a difference, try an Alderney, sold at Alderney's Channel Jumper shop, near Braye Harbour.

PERFUME & COSMETICS

St Peter Port is full of perfumeries with expensive, named brands offered – everything from Estée Lauder to Chanel. There are also a few smaller, chemist-style outlets that offer less expensive options.

Children

Guernsey, Herm, Sark and Alderney welcome children, but remember that the islands enjoy a leisurely way of life – the term 'rushing about' is not in the usual vocabulary. Children won't necessarily find attractions such as theme parks and fairs, but they will find lots of sporting activities, such as swimming, go-karting, horse riding and tennis, as well as traditional holiday pursuits like beachcombing. Guernsey, Herm, Sark and Alderney are also full of interest for children who take a shine to history and archaeology.

⬤ *Guernsey is a good destination for a family beach holiday*

TOP ACTIVITIES

Remember those childhood seaside holidays full of rock pools and sandcastles? Guernsey's beaches are the perfect place to relive those simple, old-fashioned pleasures. Armed with buckets and spades and shrimping nets, children can have days of cost-free fun. Tidal seawater pools, such as that at La Valette in St Peter Port, or the Venus Pool on Sark, offer sheltered bathing for older children.

Guernsey's coastal fortresses and museums make special efforts to appeal to all ages. Don't miss **Castle Cornet** (see page 18), especially when the noonday gun is fired, and the shipwreck museum in **Fort Grey** (see page 32). **Sausmarez Manor** (see page 38) offers a miniature railway, pets and putting. Older children might also find **La Valette Underground Military Museum** (see page 20) and the **German Occupation Museum** (see page 34) interesting.

The National Trust's Folk Museum at **Saumarez Park** (see page 29) and the **Victorian Shop** (🅰 26 Cornet Street, St Peter Port) both have child appeal. The **Beau Séjour Centre** (🅰 Amherst, St Peter Port ☎ 01481 747200) offers plenty of sports and a fine swimming pool, plus a cinema and special summer events. Check out the **Little Chapel**, a child-proportioned shrine covered with mosaics of shells and pottery (see pages 36–7), and **Guernsey's Aquarium** (in one of La Vallette's tunnels) is entrancing (☎ 01481 723301 🕐 10.00–18.00 Mon–Sat, 10.00–17.00 Sun). **The Track**, just outside St Peter Port (🅰 Victoria Avenue ☎ 01481 723414), offers go-karting 🚫 Closed Mon

EXCURSIONS

Guernsey offers the best choice of island-hopping destinations, with Herm and Sark just offshore, and Alderney within relatively easy reach. Jersey is a good excursion, too, while France seems a mere stone's throw away. Channel Island waters can be very choppy, especially around Sark, so choose a calm day.

If you're planning a visit to Alderney, a trip in one of Aurigny's tiny canary-coloured Trislander planes is a real adventure for children. Look out for Joey, the star of the fleet with the red nose and big eyes.

Festivals & events

Guernsey and the islands, especially Sark and Alderney, love festivals, carnivals and special events, and are host to many throughout the year. Some of the biggest annual events are listed opposite, although you'll find many other things going on.

Precise dates vary from year to year, so check with the tourist office. Most are geared to the main holiday season (Easter to October). Besides the normal public holidays observed in the UK, the Channel Islands commemorate Liberation Day (9 May – the end of German Occupation) and Remembrance Sunday (mid-November) with fervour. Alderney takes its August bank holiday on the first Monday of the month, as part of its Alderney Week celebrations. Alderney also celebrates Homecoming Day on 15 December, to mark the return of its inhabitants after the mass evacuation of the island in 1940. The smaller islands have summer carnivals and shows, too.

● *A young clown at Guernsey's carnival*

GUERNSEY

- Floral Festival Week (April)
- Guernsey Literary Festival (May)
- Festival of Comedy (June): stand-up shows at various venues
- Viaer Marchi (July): a traditional open-air market in Saumarez Park
- Town Carnival (July): parades and events in St Peter Port
- Battle of Flowers (August): colourful parades and a less lavish version of Jersey's big do
- Victor Hugo International Music Festival (September). Every two years. The next is in 2012
- Guernsey Jazz Festival (September)
- Guernsey Festival (October): arts events all over the island
- Tennerfest (October): a food festival during which many restaurants offer low set-menu prices
- Floral Festival (October)

ALDERNEY

- Milk-a-Punch Sunday (May): free milk and rum cocktails dispensed by local pubs
- Alderney Week (August): classic carnival scenes, with fancy dress parades, children's races and tug-of-war contests, with bonfires and fireworks to follow
- Annual Sprint, Motor and Hillclimb (September)
- Angling Festival (October)

SARK

- Midsummer Show (June): flower and produce stalls
- Folk Festival (July)
- Water Carnival (July): raft races and jolly japes in Le Creux Harbour
- Autumn Show (August): agricultural livestock and produce
- Horse Show (September): horse and carriage contest and races

Sports & activities

Guernsey offers a wide range of organised sports facilities. The Beau Séjour in St Peter Port is the largest and provides one-stop fitness in the form of swimming pools, tennis and squash courts. There's a surprising amount of sporting activity on Alderney. Famous cricketing residents, such as Ian Botham and the late John Arlott, have generated a keen interest in the crack of leather on willow.

Other active passions among its residents include homing pigeons, a ladies' darts league, bell-ringing, bowls and badminton, diving, clay-

⬤ *Riding the surf*

pigeon shooting, motor sports and aviation. Visitors are always welcome
to join in. Predictably, the smallest islands expect you to make your own
arrangements for keeping in shape. With walking on Herm or cycling on
Sark the only practical ways to explore, that isn't too difficult. These
activities are immensely popular on the other islands, too; excellent
walking and cycling booklets and maps are available from the tourist
offices containing suggested routes and information.

BOWLS
Lawn bowls can be played in several locations on Guernsey, including
outdoor bowls at Beau Séjour, and indoors at Hougue du Pommier and
Fort Regent.

FISHING
Channel Island waters attract a wide range of species of fish. Sea and
wreck-fishing boats can also be chartered on most of the islands. Ask at
the tourist offices for further details.

GOLF
The enthusiasm for harrying small white balls into tiny holes knows no
bounds on the Channel Islands. So many courses have sprung up that it's
surprising they don't overlap. Egged on by resident golfing millionaires,
Guernsey now has a number of greens, not counting numerous
pitch-and-putt and mini-golf courses. Guernsey's most popular golf club
is the Royal Guernsey at L'Ancresse Bay. Two hotel-based courses at
La Grande Mare in Vazon Bay, and St Pierre Park (designed by Tony
Jacklin) cater for the overspill. Sausmarez Manor has an enjoyable nine-
hole pitch-and-putt course in its beautiful grounds. Alderney also has a
challenging nine-hole course, with low green fees.

HORSE RIDING
Numerous schools on Guernsey offer tuition and escorted hacking.
Tourist offices can supply lists of riding schools and racing fixtures.

MOTOR SPORTS

Sand-racing, hill-climbing, rallies and motocross events are organised at various times throughout the year on Guernsey. The Guernsey Information Centre on North Esplanade, St Peter Port, is the best place to find out what's happening (☎ 01481 723552 ⓦ www.visitguernsey.com).

RACQUET SPORTS

Tennis, squash and badminton courts can be hired at the main sports complexes. Alderney also has a tennis club.

SAILING

The ritzy marinas around the Channel Islands soon tell you these waters represent nirvana for many yachtsfolk. If you're not lucky enough to own some ocean-going gin palace, you can always hire one: skippered or bareboat.

WATERSPORTS

With all that sea on the doorstep, it's hardly surprising that there's plenty for waterbabies to do. Windsurfing enthusiasts should head to Cobo and L'Ancresse bays on Guernsey for tuition or equipment. Diving is an attractive proposition in the clear waters around the Channel Islands, but you should take advice about currents. Wreck diving is a speciality. There is a diving centre in Havelet Bay on Guernsey. For novices, surfing here should probably remain a spectator sport, but experienced surfers may like to pit their skill against the Atlantic breakers of Vazon Bay in Guernsey. Other watery activities include canoeing, rowing, pedalos, jet-skiing, parascending, speedboating and 'banana boats' – available from the main watersports centre at Havelet Bay on Guernsey. Island RIB Voyages offer trips (suitable for all ages) around Guernsey and the other islands in rigid inflatable boats (☎ 01481 713031 ⓦ www.islandribvoyages.com).

▶ *One of Guernsey's distinctive blue postboxes*

PRACTICAL INFORMATION
Tips & advice

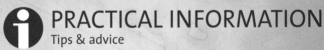

Accommodation

There are no serious luxury hotels on Guernsey, but plenty of mid-range and budget places. There are many guest houses, B&Bs and self-catering options on all the islands. The best place to get further information about these is Ⓦ www.visitguernsey.com. The hotels below are graded by approximate price:

£ budget   **££** mid-range   **£££** expensive

Abbey Court £ One of the best budget choices on the island, in a residential area, with recently refurbished rooms. ⓐ Les Gravées, St Peter Port ① 01481 720148 Ⓦ www.abbeycourthotelci.com

Bella Luce £–££ Recently renovated, old-fashioned charm in a good location, with its own grounds and a popular restaurant. ⓐ La Fosse, St Martin ① 01481 238764 Ⓦ www.bellalucehotel.guernsey.net

La Collinette ££ A good, comfortable choice in St Peter Port: near the Guernsey Museum, and a 15-minute walk to the harbour. The hotel has a lively bar, a pool, parking and a good Moroccan restaurant. La Collinette also offers self-catering apartments. ⓐ St Jacques, St Peter Port ① 01481 710331 Ⓦ www.lacollinette.com

Fleur du Jardin ££ Under new management, this old farmhouse has been refurbished to high and very stylish standards. Excellent food, friendly staff, a pool, two bars and an attractive terrace and garden. ⓐ Kings Mill, Castel ① 01481 257996

Moores ££ Very near the harbour, and surrounded by shops and eateries, this old granite house – with a bar, a restaurant, a popular Austrian-style patisserie, and fitness facilities – couldn't be better located in the island's capital. ⓐ Le Pollet, St Peter Port ① 01481 724452 Ⓦ www.moores. sarniahotels.com

La Trelade ££ Pleasantly furnished and well-equipped rooms, an indoor pool, small gym, a sauna and a conservatory restaurant. ⓐ Forest Road, St Martin ❶ 01481 235454 ⓦ www.latreladehotel.co.uk

Farmhouse Hotel ££–£££ Modern décor in this very comfortable family-run hotel. Also four dining areas with wide-ranging menus, an outdoor pool and garden. ⓐ Rue des Bas Courtils, St Saviour ❶ 01481 264181 ⓦ www.thefarmhouse.gg

La Frégate ££–£££ This boutique hotel, with fine views, good facilities and one of the best restaurants on the island, is one of the top upmarket addresses on Guernsey. ⓐ Les Cotils, St Peter Port ❶ 01481 724624 ⓦ www.lafregatehotel.com

La Grande Mare ££–£££ Set in spacious grounds (including a golf course and tennis court) with fine views of Vazon Bay. The hotel also boasts well-decorated rooms, health facilities and has a good restaurant, as well as indoor and outdoor pools. ⓐ Vazon Bay, Castel ❶ 01481 256576 ⓦ www.lgm.guernsey.net

Fermain Valley Hotel £££ In a pretty valley location near the coast, a very good hotel with two high-quality restaurants, terraces with fine views, an indoor pool and a private cinema. ⓐ Fermain Bay, St Martin ❶ 01481 235666 ⓦ www.fermainvalley.com

Old Government House £££ The former residence of Guernsey's governors is now arguably the island's best hotel, offering high levels of service and comfort, as well as two restaurants and leisure facilities, including a spa and pool. Many rooms have sea views. ⓐ St Ann's Place, St Peter Port ❶ 01481 724981 ⓦ www.theoghhotel.com

PRACTICAL INFORMATION

Preparing to go

GETTING THERE

By far the best way to visit Guernsey is as part of an inclusive
package, although travelling independently by booking a flight and
accommodation is popular, too. Guernsey is well served by airlines, and
there are regular flights from airports in the UK, including Birmingham,
Southampton, Gatwick, Stansted, Exeter, Manchester and Norwich.
Flying time is normally around an hour. Travelling by sea to Jersey is
easy from Poole, Portsmouth and Weymouth. For information on tour
operators featuring Guernsey, visit Ⓦ www.abta.com

Airlines include:
Aurigny Air Services Also inter-island flights to Alderney and Jersey.
Ⓣ 0871 871 0717 Ⓦ www.aurigny.com
Blue Islands Also inter-island flights to Alderney and Jersey.
Ⓣ 01481 727567 Ⓦ www.blueislands.com
Flybe From many airports around Britain. Ⓣ 0871 522 6100
Ⓦ www.flybe.com

Many people are aware that air travel emits CO_2, which contributes to
climate change. You may be interested in the possibility of lessening the
environmental impact of your flight through the charity **Climate Care**,
which offsets your CO_2 by funding environmental projects around the
world. Visit Ⓦ www.jpmorganclimatecare.com

Ferry operators:
Condor Ferries From the South Coast of England. Ⓣ 0870 243 5140
Ⓦ www.condorferries.com
Isle of Sark Shipping Company Ⓦ www.sarkshipping.info

TOURISM AUTHORITY

Guernsey's main tourist office is at the Guernsey Information Centre,
North Esplanade, St Peter Port. Ⓣ 01481 723552 Ⓦ www.visitguernsey.com